What the Small Day
Cannot Hold

Also by Susan Musgrave

Fiction
The Charcoal Burners (1980)
The Dancing Chicken (1990)

Poetry
Songs of the Sea-Witch (1970)
Entrance of the Celebrant (1972)
Grave-Dirt and Selected Strawberries (1973)
The Impstone (1976)
Kiskatinaw Songs (with Seán Virgo, 1978)
Selected Strawberries and Other Poems (1977)
Becky Swan's Book (1977)
A Man to Marry, a Man to Bury (1979)
Tarts and Muggers: Poems New and Selected (1982)
Cocktails at the Mausoleum (1985)
The Embalmer's Art: Poems New and Selected (1991)
Forcing the Narcissus (1994)
Things That Keep and Do Not Change (1999)

Children's
Gullband (1973)
Hag Head (1980)
Kestrel and Leonardo (1990)
Dreams Are More Real Than Bathtubs (1999)

Nonfiction
Great Musgrave (1988)
Musgrave Landing: Musings on the Writing Life (1991)

Compiled and Edited
Clear-Cut Words: Writers for Clayoquot (1993)
Because You Loved Being a Stranger: 55 Poets Celebrate Patrick Lane (1994)

What the Small Day Cannot Hold

Collected Poems 1970-1985

SUSAN MUSGRAVE

Introduction by Seán Virgo

Porcepic Books
an imprint of

Beach Holme Publishing
Vancouver

This book is published by Beach Holme Publishing, #226—2040 West
12th Ave., Vancouver, BC, V6J 2G2. This is a Porcepic Book.

We acknowledge the financial support
of the Canada Council for the Arts, the
Government of Canada through the Book
Publishing Industry Development Program
(BPIDP) and the assistance of the Province
of British Columbia through the British
Columbia Arts Council for our publishing
activities and program.

The Canada Council | Le Conseil des Arts
for the Arts | du Canada

Editor: Michael Carroll
Production and Design: Jen Hamilton
Cover Art: Christiane Pflug, *Kitchen Door with Esther*, 1965, 64" x 76", oil
on canvas. Estate of the Artist. Used with permission of Michael Pflug.
Photo courtesy of Art Gallery of Ontario.

Canadian Cataloguing in Publication Data

Musgrave, Susan, 1951-
  What the small day cannot hold

  ISBN 0-88878-406-6

  I. Title.
PS8576.U7W44 2000   C811'.54   C00-910083-0
PR9199.3.M84W44 2000

To Stephen—these years harder than ever

Contents

Grave-Dirt and Selected Strawberries   79

The Impstone

Cocktails at the Mausoleum

Acknowledgements

I wish to thank the following publishers of the first editions of the books that comprise this collection of my poetry: Sono Nis Press (*Songs of the Sea-Witch*, 1970); Macmillan Canada/England's Fuller d'Arch Smith (*Entrance of the Celebrant*, 1972); Macmillan Canada (*Grave-Dirt and Selected Strawberries*, 1973); McClelland & Stewart (*The Impstone*, 1976, and *A Man to Marry, a Man to Bury*, 1979); The Porcupine's Quill (*Becky Swan's Book*, 1977); and McClelland & Stewart/Beach Holme Publishing (*Cocktails at the Mausoleum*, 1985 and 1992).

I would also like to thank the editors of the following magazines and anthologies in which some of the poems in this collection first appeared: **Canada:** *Ariel, Arts Manitoba, Aurora: Canadian Writing 1978, Aurora: Canadian Writing 1980, Benchmarks, Books in Canada, Branching Out, Canadian Forum, Canadian Literature, The Capilano Review, Cloud Nine: Vancouver Island Poems, Contemporary Fiction of British Columbia, Contemporary Poetry of British Columbia Volume II, Cross-Canada Writers' Quarterly, CV2, Descant, Dialog, D'sonoqua: An Anthology of Women Poets of British Columbia, Echo, end of the world speshul, Event, Exile, Far Point, The Fiddlehead, The Fireweed Collection, First Encounter, Gamut, Grail, The Headless Angel, Impulse, Light in Darkness, Makara, The Malahat Review, Manna, Mindscapes, Mirror Northwest, New West Coast, Northern Journey, Northern Light, Quarry, Poetry Canada Review, The Poets of Canada, Prism international, Queen's Quarterly, Raincoast Chronicles, The Red Cedar Review, Revue, Room of One's Own, Saturday Night, The Tamarack Review, Tawow, Toronto Life, Treeline II, Tributaries, True North Down Under, Tuatara, Twelf Key #0, #1, #2, University College Review, Waves, West Coast Review, Western Windows, Women's Eye, Women Poets: Canada*, and *Writing*; **United States:** *The Black Cat, Fear and Fearlessness, Modern Poetry Studies, Mundus Artium, Negative Capability, New Orleans Review, The Niagara Magazine, South Shore, Temple University Poetry Newsletter, Three Rivers Poetry Journal*, and *West Coast Poetry Review*; **England:** *Aquarius, Bananas, Contrasts, Expression, The Little Word Machine,*

New Departures, Oasis, Poetry Review, Prospice, Second Aeon, Slow Dancer, Trends, Wordworks, and *Workshop*; **Australia:** *Helix* and *Poetry Australia.*

I am grateful to Robert Graves and to Faber & Faber for permission to use the quotations from *The White Goddess* that appear as section headings in the first four parts of *Songs of the Sea-Witch.* Many of the poems in *Entrance of the Celebrant* have been broadcast on CBC's *Anthology* in Canada, and on the BBC's *The Third Programme* in England. The poems in the second section of *Grave-Dirt and Selected Strawberries* were selected from *Kiskatinaw Songs,* a book written in collaboration with Seán Virgo and Moses Bruce. A number of poems from *Grave-Dirt* were broadcast on CBC's *Anthology.* I am grateful, in the writing of *The Impstone,* to the Masset Band Council for permission to visit the abandoned villages of Kung and Yatza, and to the Skidegate Band Council for permission to visit Kaisun.

For the titles of certain poems in this collection, I am indebted to the following people. In *Entrance of the Celebrant:* "The Night, the Real Night..."—Randal Jarrell. In *The Impstone:* "It Is a True Error to Marry with Poets"—John Berryman; "The Babies Are Growing into Their Suits"—Mark Strand; "It's Hard to Be Kind to a Cannibal"—Haidée Virgo. In *A Man to Marry, a Man to Bury:* "What the Small Day Cannot Hold"—Frances Bellerby; "Dig, He Said, Dig"—Louis MacNeice; "Recognition Not Enough"—Stevie Smith. *In Cocktails at the Mausoleum:* "And on the Coming of the Outrageous Dawn"—Frances Bellerby; "Exile Is in Our Time Like Blood..."—John Berryman; "& the great white horses come up & lick the frost of the dream"—Charles Bukowski; "Conversation During the Omelette Aux Fines Herbes"—Cynthia MacDonald; "I Do Not Know If Things That Happen Can Be Said to Come to Pass or Only Happen"—Howard Nemerov.

Susan Musgrave
Sidney, British Columbia
February 2000

Introduction
The Subversive Art of Susan Musgrave

by Seán Virgo

cunning and art she did not lack

The poetry is the only thing about Susan Musgrave more subversive than herself. It is dramatic, visionary, ironic and unteachable. And there's the thing: if our academics and reviewers—the "fleas upon the body poetic"—could reduce the poetry to teachable, "relevant" or ideological paraphrase, they might be able to acknowledge it as the most original work of our time. But then, of course, it wouldn't be if they could.

In a tiny piece of coloured glass
My love was born

The opening lines to Donovan Leitch's song "Jersey Thursday" were the first poetry I ever heard from Susan Musgrave's lips. It was 1968, and she was seventeen.

The details of her interesting life at that time are common knowledge. So are the details of her interesting life to this day— she has found "more enterprise in walking naked", and that's the essence of her subversiveness: for the unspeakable or unbearable become in her hands strangely complex and vulnerably human, and unbelievers are moved to revise their moralities.

Troubled teenager, cuckoo in the nest, runaway, ward-of-court, acid freak, marriage breaker, hospital inmate for a spell. Those facts are approximately true, concealing still other realities. Yet angels recognized and attended Musgrave even then: a math teacher who let her write poems in the back of his class, and predicted her future achievements; a social worker who bent every imaginable rule in her favour; and, most famously, the poet Robin Skelton, who barged into a Victoria psych ward to announce that she was not mad, but a poet—or "poyt", as Skelton characteristically pronounced it and Musgrave, just as characteristically, mimicked.

In person, as in her writing, Musgrave has always been a fond parodist, with an eye and ear not just for quirks of expression, cadence and delivery, but for the human quiddities that they conceal. Alienated teenager she may have been, breaker of social taboos and parents' hearts, but her repertoire at that time was full of her family's quirks, going back two generations. They enshrined her Musgrave-Stevens heritage, not least in its Anglo-Irish penchant for rash and eccentric stubbornness ("you didn't fit," she would write for her father years later after his death). They were loving, and hilarious. We shall hear them down the road, echoing through her poems.

Angels of another kind walked with her shadow back then, and continue to do so. At least they are as good an explanation as any for her gift of serendipity—in life as in language. Runestones on the beach, old books on a library shelf, artifacts at the back of a shop window came to her as the words did: as though patient, unremarked parts of the visible world called out to her to recognize and complete them, so that they in turn might help to realize her. Treasure trove. Word hoard as well, of course.

Throughout that time, whatever the company she was in, the confusions that beset her or the troubles that she risked, she was listening to music and writing, writing, writing.

By the fall of 1969, her first book of poems, *Songs of the Sea-Witch*, would be accepted for publication. And I come back to those lines that she quoted from Donovan, as a starting point for understanding her early work. Why were they one of her treasures? Because, I think, they are not a metaphor; they are a statement of actual experience.

> *I won't be*
> *ready until all the world is ready; I*
> *want to see it all at once*

Being eighteen years old in 1969 in Victoria, British Columbia, was to wake up each day to the option of adventure.

There was squalor enough in the counterculture, but there was optimism, too—a tolerance for originality, a hunger for the new and exotic. Canadian youth was on the road in huge numbers, maple leaves adorned rucksacks all over Europe, Asia and South America.

Kids were genuinely interested in ideas, however half-baked or half-digested. Alan Watts, Norman O. Brown, R. D. Laing and Abraham Maslow wrote the commonplace books. Enlightenment might be found in the "white light at the back of my mind", the final LSD ecstasy; the cure for society's ills might be found in other cultures, distant in time or space.

The *I-Ching* was consulted, transcendental meditation explored, the lyrics of popular songs turned into oracles. And the cycle of interest in the occult was coming round, not yet formalized into the coziness of Wicca or the pseudo-feminism of "goddess worship".

If the background was the war in Vietnam, someone else's problem, we should not forget that Canada gave haven to countless Americans of conscience. The "draft dodgers" and the stifled young academics brought with them the spirit of rebellion, and a grab-bag of philosophies, psychologies, poetries, musics and religions that challenged almost everything.

Them and Us seemed for a brief spell to be not a class definition but a philosophical one. Us, of course, was clearly in the right.

The enemy were the establishment, big business, the Pentagon, the narcs.

Pierre Elliott Trudeau was going to legalize pot.

"Johnny, please come home. You can wear your hair long."

All we needed was Love, and to give Peace a chance.

> It's my way of talking to the world
> when I say I wear a wig of blood and my
> eyes are as hollow as your cerebral passage

The poetic climate on the West Coast then was varied, to say the least. Silver-haired Earle Birney was reading to flower children at love-ins: "How can I learn you/Is there a map of you?" and chanting choo-choo-train poems; bill bissett was chanting, too, running blewointmentpress and spelling words the way he, at least, heard them; Patrick Lane was emerging as a tighter, fiercer successor to Al Purdy. (The women, except for Dorothy Livesay, were quieter: P. K. Page and Phyllis Webb did marvellous work but kept their own counsel.) As for the universities, there was the English tradition in Victoria; a Black Mountain enclave at Simon Fraser; a surrealist faction at UBC. And there was J. Michael Yates, a Missouri hothead who galvanized a cabal of young poets in UBC's Graduate School and who, as the founder of Sono Nis Press, was Musgrave's first publisher.

There were also, of course, in almost everyone's ears, Bob Dylan, Leonard Cohen, Joni Mitchell, Jim Morrison, Buffy Sainte-Marie, Donovan, the Stones, the Beatles, Pink Floyd, Procol Harum, Led Zeppelin, Jefferson Airplane...

You had to be really original to be original.

My mind is a speck of sound
within a silent universe

Songs of the Sea-Witch creates a world that reflects and contains the human drama that animates it. (That's god-language, I suppose, but nonetheless true.) In part, the terrain is recognizable as the forest, rivers and beaches of the Northwest Coast, but these spaces are haunted, and shifting: they are a stage as much as a landscape. The reader does not breathe familiar air, though, and watch from the gallery. To enter this world, the reader must enter the speaker.

That is what I meant by saying, from the start, that Musgrave's poetry is dramatic—with her first four books at least, we must often, as readers, abandon our own skins. The poems are not addressed *to* us, or even spoken for us to eavesdrop upon; they begin to work when we make their voice our own.

It is an outraged, wondering voice in this instance, engaged in the exorcism of loss and betrayal, falling back into solitude and finding strength there, as well as grief.

There is a lover here, only half the magician he promised to be, always slipping away to the forest, always tugged by his love for another woman, never paying enough attention to the world he was meant to complete. He is a magician, an executioner, a hunter, a competitive fake, a failure.

There are almost unbearable scenes of betrayal (as in part two of the title poem), visions born out of the damned pornography that is jealousy, and there are threats that are as sad and self-condemning as they are vicious ("I will betray you, my lover,/I will ruin you./I will smash my rotten destestable heart/on all the preoccupation/of your mind"); but the vividness of the images, and the (mostly) unforced, unexpected turns of language and cadence give the book's wounded world a luminosity that is as much dream as nightmare. The exorcist has no desire to escape this world entirely: she knows, "There is/danger in sanity/there is danger/in sanity/there is danger/in not understanding loss."

Any good actor would recognize the potential in the above quotations. The phrasing and cadence are perfect, but they are no straitjacket: they offer as many interpretive options for the voice as "Miss Julie's crazy again tonight" or "Get thee to a nunnery."

An actor—or the chameleon reader I have prescribed—will also discover a variety of tones in *Songs of the Sea-Witch* that my brief summary does not suggest and which, I know, contemporary readers did not recognize. You cannot read, out loud, lines like "There were birds there, my love/and a music box that/sang if I wanted it to—/at first I thought it was/all quite nice/but then I discovered/the shredded bones of people/half-lost in feathers..." and not find yourself dealing with three totally different moods: fairy-tale enchantment, near-Gothic horror and, bridging them, that "at first I thought it was all quite nice", which is, of course, a mocking, middle-class parody. The subversive wit is never absent from the poetry at any stage of Musgrave's career, though it is so often overlooked.

Nevertheless, an obsessive imagery of bones, the dead, ghosts and "old men with blood in their hair", does dominate the better part of the book, along with the elemental, vaguely animate presence of roots, trees and stones. It is a dreamscape, certainly (Musgrave always insisted "the blood in my poems is not real blood"—"but the unhappened moment/is real blood"), but it is not, therefore, to be dismissed or decoded. There are societies still in the world for whom dreams are every bit as real as waking experience, where "it was just a dream" would be meaningless as consolation or denial.

We must take the visions literally, if we can. And follow the young poet as she explores, in her next three books, different modes and stages of transformation. It is a human, as well as a poetic apprenticeship. Hence the epigraphs from Robert Graves's version of Alison Gowdie's seventeenth-century witch-trial confession. And hence the Sea Witch herself (whether we read her as the main speaker, or as the mysterious bisexual visitant who "rose on the tide line" the "mistress of nettles" whose "laughter was yours.")

The witchery is not melodrama. It is—at the risk of sounding willfully paradoxical—the discipline of reaching across time and space to discover oneself.

> *It is not*
> *deliverance—I believe in the*
> *life we die into*

Musgrave's still-interesting life evolved, for the next three years, in Ireland and England. She had to be affected, as anyone from the New World is, by the density of the air there, the sense of history cloaking the land, the almost claustrophobic presence of the past. And her obsessive writing was replaced, to some extent, by obsessive reading.

More conscious of herself now as a writer, learning to decode the reactions of other writers, distinguishing between responses to her as "young, blond and beautiful", or as genuine, original poet, she must, as a high-school dropout, have felt her ignorance, especially in the company of articulate, opinionated English friends.

But I think she raided her friends' knowledge store for what she could use, and her reading followed that chain reaction that most writers know: where a book falls out of a library shelf into your hands, and something you find there leads you away down a seemingly preordained trail. Her serendipitous angels were at work.

If her new writing was less "language at war with itself" (Michael Yates's phrase for the work he most valued by her), it was learning new games with line, punctuation and tense that replaced atmospheric imagery with dramatic shorthand, as seen in "Night and Fog" in *Entrance of the Celebrant*:

> Voices I called to
> out of the blind fog
> drew me that way.

Into the wet woods
calling them: they do not
answer and I am
possessed again.

Published in England and Canada in 1972, *Entrance of the Celebrant* takes its title from Igor Stravinsky's *Rites of Spring* and suggests the conscious connection the poems are making between the rituals of poetry and the ancestors, spirits and creatures who may link us to the elements. The speaker (and, again, the reader must take on that persona) is, in effect, a priest or shaman, privy—if only as spy—to the otherworld mysteries. We see Skuld, the Elf-Queen, in her "forest where the dead go", and peer into the holy of holies:

Down in the dimly lit passage
a simple light burns. It is
the Queen's heart returning
to her cold breast.

The language is confident and matter-of-factly magical. (Although it is worth recording that Musgrave's favourite, derisive parody at that time was of people who called her work, or anything else, "truly magical".)

Initiation, though, is involvement—listening, hearing, attending: "The dead come in the evening/bringing their messages gathered into/dreams"; it is empathy: "The dead dream of dying, too"; and beyond this, it is the process of actual transformation. We enter one of Goya's witchcraft etchings, *Disparates*, and discover the truth of which he shows only the surface:

I am this shape

          of *this* woman or
these five women tugging at rags
tossing the twisted
animal skin inside them,
pulling me always from the centre
out.

Again, the lines are used with wonderful skill: read them the way they should be heard and you suffer the labour pangs of rebirth. This rebirth, culminating in the title poem, is the recovery of the animal self we have lost. We retain our human, even our erotic definitions but "No one forgets/the music of the animal. I've heard/the sound of the old skin cracking/where this heart has become/the heart of something new."

Hum ke pupum! Ha!

The Old World hath its charms, but it is very easy to miss Canada in the damp winter of an English fenland city where central heating is a rumoured Yankee indulgence, and you can't even find pickles or peanut butter in the stores. By early spring, Musgrave was on her way back across the Atlantic, heading for the Queen Charlotte Islands—the spiritual heartland, in a mythic sense at least, of the pre-Contact Northwest Coast.

It was not just homesickness. Those voices in the blind fog had begun to answer her call. In fact, they had taken over her life in the last few months: raunchy ancestral voices that chanted and raved and were very human indeed.

Despite its climate, Cambridge had treasures to offer. One place of refuge was the Museum of Ethnology, with its radiator heat and a glorious jumble of loot from the British Empire and beyond. There were feathers and bones and stones enough here: Moctezuma's feather cloak, shrunken heads from the Amazon, swollen heads from Melanesia, a Dakota warrior's hand made into a medicine pouch. But in one glass case, in their own exile, were artifacts brought back to England by Captain Cook's Nootka expedition, two hundred years away from home.

The *Kiskatinaw Songs* began.

There are transformation poems among them: ghostly, shamanic figures, half-human, half-animal ("Frogs whistled/In the rock-throat of the/Mountain, sea-lice were clinging/To his sides"), but the majority speak from the childhood of mankind, often in nursery-rhyme cadence, from a world before the Fall when sex was not shameful, neurotic or glamorous, but extremely interesting:

> You must play the
> Lip-biting.
> You must play the
> Right Way.
> You must play at
> Belly-rubbing.
> Because I like to watch.

The poems are charged with sexuality, shaped by the rhythms of incantation (two favourite books at that time were *Shaking the Pumpkin* and *Technicians of the Sacred*), and full of mischief.

Kiskatinaw Songs formed the second of three sections in *Grave-Dirt and Selected Strawberries*, a new collection published in 1973 by Macmillan. The cover of the book featured a monochrome Gustave Doré etching of a necromancer, dealing out her "wicked pack of cards", surrounded by skulls and corkindrells, with a headless skeleton in attendance. The skeleton cradles a massive red strawberry.

No one in Canada was going to get away with calling Musgrave "truly magical".

> *I taught the*
> *Prince of Darkness*
> *to say his prayers*

There is, in fact, some quite potent magic in the "Grave-Dirt" section *of Grave-Dirt and Selected Strawberries*, continuing both the under-cover shamanic espionage of *Entrance of the Celebrant* and the folkloric cantations of *Kiskatinaw Songs*, but probably the most interesting poems are the two sequences, "One-Sided Woman" and "The Metempsychosis of Satan Bragg". A new kind of drama is at work here: via terse, ironic facets of the two lives, the reader is offered distilled narratives, with commentary, to observe rather than to enter. Now we enjoy the storyteller, for her inventiveness ("her face like a/gargoyle on a/picnic/breaking open/more eggs/than were ever meant/to be eaten") and for her sardonic analogies:

> Their marriage was like a
> stuffed bird

sleeping with
one eye
open

Simile and metaphor are becoming part of Musgrave's vocabulary
as they never were before: the vision is not now insisted upon as
a luminous reality—it is offered as something to be interpreted.

With "Selected Strawberries", too, we are very aware of the
poet as entertainer. They are almost entirely lighthearted pieces
(though "A Child's Garden of Strawberries" is a weirdly evocative,
sinister poem, as disturbing, for me, as anything she had written
to date). The sequence is a miscellany of parodies, inversions and
elegant pastiches, reflecting the amazingly disparate range of
books that had been devoured in the past five years.

Her interesting life continued.

Yesterday
I loved you
today well
I don't know

The Impstone, in 1976, is also three books in one. The opening
section lays to rest a lifestyle, a relationship and an aesthetic, sadly
and consciously. These are very beautiful poems, with the familiar
imagery of elements, animals and spirits, but the language and
verse forms have a new poise and precision, and the ghosts live
in a time dimension, rather than on another plane ("I saw our
ghosts/making love/under the trees"). It is worth comparing these
poems to those in *Songs of the Sea-Witch* and seeing how much
more human they are. Outrage and exorcism have given way to
sorrow and farewell.

But in the next section, "Recovery" (and its John Berryman
epigraph, "O and a gash..."), a new energy begins, with a racier,
more colloquial language, and a willingness to include the contem-
porary, material world as the subject of poetry. Deadpan anecdotes
result, with a cast of real people: "I think of/Al and Eurithe at/
a party in/Progreso. Al got/drunk and left his/bathing suit
behind./Could have happened/to anyone."), and there are strange

impersonations of other voices, too: "Remember taking off your/ clothes in the/woods—goddamn/it makes me feel/desperate, you were so/tight." The poetic strength is now a matter of timing, shaping, juxtaposing. And just as the ironic and parodic tone used to undercut the seriousness of Musgrave's early poetry, now the dark and transformative notes subvert the chatty surfaces of her language.

"Archaeologists and Graverobbers", though, the closing sequence of poems for the half-submerged Haida culture, reminds us that voices do not change completely overnight. Here the shamanic mode continues to develop, and will find its most powerful expression six years later in "Requiem for Talunkwun Island".

Nor had the witches been left behind altogether.

> *Ah but some women like that are*
> *wicked. Some women are wicked*

Ancestral West Coast voices had called through the Cambridgeshire mists; now an English voice from another time, intimate, gossipy, scandalized, insisted on being heard. *Becky Swan's Book* is Musgrave's most purely dramatic work: a coven of poems that an actor must some day adapt. The voice, distinctive as it is, cries out to be fleshed out, interpreted. Perhaps one can hear the influence of the English poet Stevie Smith in some of the cadences (perhaps Musgrave's beloved English Great Aunt Polly had something to do with this, too), but essentially we are hearing a perfectly mad woman, from a village world that is as on fire with devilry and suspicion as Salem, Massachusetts, ever was.

Is Becky Swan a malicious peeper through walls and lace curtains, a frustrated spinster with a wild fantasy life, a genuine visionary, or simply crazy? No doubt the same questions could have been asked of most women taken as witches in the sixteenth and seventeenth centuries.

And taken she apparently was. For when *Becky Swan's Book* was included in the 1979 collection *A Man to Marry, a Man to Bury*, another poem, "Witchfinder General", confides that Isobel Long and Rebecca Swan, the "lonely old crones", were tortured, staked and burned.

> *Man, I gotta do somethin about old Charlie.*
> *Man, I gotta do somethin.*

By the time *A Man to Marry, a Man to Bury* was published in 1979, Musgrave had a sense of an actual audience for her work—not her readership, but the crowds who attended her public readings. Her skills, both as performer and raconteuse, were and are phenomenal, and as she developed them her gifts as a mimic and her instinct for drama embraced all the worlds that her interesting life had touched. They now became the subject matter of her poetry.

It is a different kind of drama, another mode of transformation altogether.

There is always something comical about mimicry, but it can be used at the same time for very serious ends. By taking on the voices of losers, bingo addicts, illiterates and drunks, Musgrave found styles and energies for which you can feel her genuine affection, but which also dramatize social problems that are usually preached about or ignored. It is very complex poetry, with every appearance of simple-mindedness. It is brilliant and subversive, and sometimes it gives offence. But, always insisting on the autonomy of poetry, she has shrugged off such offence with: "I let the poem have its own way... The opinions expressed are not necessarily those of the writer."

For me, though, the masterpiece in this book is "Coming of Age", a memory of "Giffey the outlaw", part-tramp, part-devil, exhibiting himself to some adolescent girls, finally impotent and pitiable before their power and knowledge:

> We were the peaty source of his
> darkness, with our lies and our smiles
> and stories about our lives.
> For there were no blessings in our cold
> eyes, only cruelty, and more of that for
> our youth.

This is subversive in the way that *A High Wind in Jamaica* is. It is also a real sign of poetic maturity when abstract language, not dependent on image, can carry such authority, make such music and create such atmosphere.

Before her next poetry collection appeared, Musgrave wrote and published a novel, *The Charcoal Burners*, and become a mother. And she travelled in Europe and Central America. There were stories to tell, and an elegy to complete.

> *I cannot tell them how life is when the*
> *soul has left it; the body does not die*
> *but how can they know that.*

I could have chosen a far racier epigraph from *Cocktails at the Mausoleum* than the lines above. It is a "rich and varied" collection, with too many strands to summarize—all pointing to Musgrave's future development, and all emerging naturally from her earlier obsessions and departures. One section chronicles, with deceptive simplicity, a reading tour in England with George Johnston and bill bissett, and includes the only good poem (except for Ann Sexton's) I have ever read about Sylvia Plath. There are poems based on dreams, poems that arise from rollicking impulse, poems that play according to their own rules. Another section draws on her interesting life with her "pirate" husband, and the self-doubt involved in writing poetry when poverty, politics and vicious military dictatorships cast doubt on it all (her unfailing irony, praise be, resolves that issue).

But I chose lines from "Requiem for Talunkwan Island" partly because it is the one strand of her work that ends naturally in 1985; mostly because I believe it is a great poem, the most eloquent threnody ever composed in Canada, both heartbreaking and cathartic.

The ghost of Haida speaks to us from the then and the now:

> Eternal life is unlivable
> yet men rut like fat bucks in the
> bush and women go sighing.
> It's a sad thing to be lonely in the
> body, but to have no body at all—
> that's the loneliest.

The voice is both human and elemental, individual and generic. I think the shamanic side of Musgrave had been circling this achievement for years, never trusting herself until now to dare the whole connection. This was the poet who had mocked herself in earlier books for her presumption ("my white skin fools them every time", and "Go back to the south and write another poem about Indians"), but in the end those islands and their spirits appropriated her voice. She would leave that piece of herself behind.

She was thirty-four years old.

We are not a poetic culture. We leave visionary work to the limp clichés of the "new age". Our taste is for documentary, for prosaic confession and anecdote, for humourless word games, or—at our best—for the spectacle of a skillful mind elaborating a thought on the page. We believe we are realists. We would fit very well into Plato's *Republic*.

Susan Musgrave is one of the few who would not. She'd survive, though, because the governors would not have the wit to see what she was about. They ought to banish her. She is so funny and charming, but charm is a conjurer's wand. Those who enter her dance discover that the wall of the Cave is not a pallid screen at all, but an entrance.

Photo by Seán Virgo

Songs of the Sea-Witch
1970

I

O, I shall go into a hare
With sorrow and sighing and mickle care,
And I shall go in the Devil's name
Aye, till I be fetchèd hame.

After the Rain

After the rain
the field gates open,
the slanting sun
trims our tired wet bones;

we scream the vowels
of freedom,
the wheel tracks freshen
as hell falls through—

by the road
grandpa finds us
unreal mushrooms,
red, brown
and orange—
an unreal grandpa
who knows the calls of all the birds,

who sings and sighs
a snail of the vain and ugliest

while our lips mould the smoke of fallen starlight
and our hearts toll like clappers
in the bell of dark.

Night Poem

Under the snow
and foxes barking,
a skull winked
　　—my grandmother saw it—

Snow on the wind
and yard lamps
blinking
　　—she could hear her footsteps
　　　on the unpaved road—

Cold dreams in the night
drilled the wet untired dark
　　—in the hour, the season
　　　she tamed them with her plough—

Ice in the well
and broken windows
　　—she would glue together
　　　the shattered pieces,
　　　set them in
　　　like precious stones—

Snow on the hill,
imaginary lane
　　—she would die first
　　　for all the others dying,
　　　carted away
　　　thick and blistered

Absent in the dust and
patient in her chair.

The Spilled Child

Now, too,
you are wanting
the spilled child out of me,
the last part
unbroken down
     —the abandoned bird
        wingless and screaming
        in a corner—

Now you too.
Down among the many dawns
bleached in iron rivers
whoring on chains
of muddy fish—
       you too
in the blackness that bites off
all the white flowers,
the darkness that meets you
everywhere
with sad news from home—
       you too
want the spilled child
to die in secret
or not at all,
to sew her body
to the ground with worms
or preen all the birds' songs
of waiting
     —the birds that drag the night
        like a black sheet
        in their beaks—

while our hearts and kidneys
crash like cymbals

—some of them were
   torn into pieces
   because of their refusal to sing—

So I will go
and in the black spring
I will pick dead flowers.
At night I will overturn stones.
Curious and broken
the spilled child
will burn
reluctantly and for a long time.

II

Yet I shall go into a trout
With sorrow and sighing and mickle doubt,
And show thee many a merry game
Ere that I be fetchèd hame.

At Nootka Sound

Along the river
trees are stranded
bare as witches
and dark as the woman
who never learned to love one man.

(In the north
a woman can learn
to live with too much sadness.
Finding *anything* could be hard.)

The river is haunted
with the slippery black eyes

of drowned pika—
you fish for something quite improbable
expecting those thin dead eyes
to begin to see.

Sometimes along the way
the water breaks
and Indians must mend the river
after every other net—
men with fat dog's eyes
and humps
who cast themselves
toward fish in stone.

What could only be one lifetime
(who can go on pretending forever?)
is when the ground turns cold
and the night is so still
you can't remember having anything to hear.
You lose yourself
and off into the distance
the last birds are throbbing
black and enormous
down toward the sea.

Mackenzie River, North

Filled with darkness
we are already late for this river.
Shadows file behind us
seeping into the light of our eyes.
The river is blind
and refuses to stay.
We move past in our silence,
a long black mile,
cast into some huge emptiness
like continents of tooth and stone.

The river is not our only hunter.
White against the road
the slow rain drives us back
against the ground.
Wolves smell us out of our bones,
fish grow bored and swim away.
There is nothing about for us
but fear

> And moving,
> always moving,
> out of the night
> it comes.

North Sea Poem

This sea carries no emblem—
I'm afraid of its harbours,
unknown water
bottled like a note that might come drifting
any minute
onto your floor.

Yet it wasn't for your love
that the birds came singing
into our hands, web-footed
on the yellow beach,
and bolted from our torches
like water out of a day of ice.

It wasn't for the waves
that your mouth was dancing,
for with them you knew
no safety was close enough.

But I can't wear this ocean,
even lend myself for a

temporary calm.
I'm just afraid
that in your madness
you'll steal out and launch another tide—
in our wake
and long before you,
a blood-pit onto some clay dry grave.

For Seán

She rose on the tide line
when I first saw her,
hair alive with shadows
dancing on ice over roots of grass

a stone
a shell
the footprint of a small bird left.

She is lady of the green,
she is your lady
lost to you.
Driven mad in the summer
she sang and sang—
there was no one
who could stop her singing.
And running wild in the woods
she seeded in the full of the moon
your heart—
pushed it behind my breast
and I breathed as you
in the dark ocean night
caught beneath your moon
caught in her laughter
that was yours—
almost then
I knew who I was.

And she
let the laughter keep on falling,
turned her pale eyes down—
    she said
    one day you will not care
    if I go away

My fingers trailing through your wake
I am already fading
    before you.

The Night Passage

She comes here
out of the water, gathering poison
idly
to feed
to different fish.
Trees root at her ankles
from every wind—
she is mistress of nettles
tearing her eyes in the dark to find
her blood run wild with knives: she is
the goddess of thorn.

And there is more. Night after night
she cannot sleep but is
pressed from hand to hand
terrified to wake
and find me gone, terrified that I will
shut her out of the dark
or leave her to finish the cold alone.

But we are dead
together—I can hear her
breathe in stone, the breath of
death-rot that rides me out to the

dark unwilling foam.
Arm in arm with the sea
so I pass the night

as she, in her last bare dance
swings in her eyes
the weight of tides
and stalks in my shadow, promising
what she kills.

Songs of the Sea-Witch

Long Beach, Vancouver Island—
Victoria, B.C. May 1969

I

Soon you will be gone
out of my life
forever—
you will put on your shoes
and your coat,
you will say

I am just leaving

that will be all

and I will weep tar
for this love of ours that should have been.

Now it is dark, my love,
O it is dark.
What alternatives do I have
after dark?
I take another lover—
for him I am more alive than others.

I come with half-mad eyes
from the soul of a bird
pounding after him
at early dawn

so mad
and so utterly lost.

Once we dreamed
of the same stone.
He is flawless, at first
so I take—
I have nothing to give
and where I shrink
each dawn from skeletons with
their knees drawn up and
old men with
blood in their hair
it is his eyes
who stagger before me
forcing me down
until I admit to
his miserable pain.

Now it is winter
and I must avoid traps.
Like a whore
I am carefree and I hurt.
Go away, I tell my lover,
I have drowned by natural causes,
my instincts say
there is grace in death.
Go back to your woman,
her mind may be cruel
but her body is warm.
I am hardly alive,
My heart is an old rag.

My bones are not sensational,
they are just there.

I am the last one left
with blood on my hands.
I want to know
where self-destruction ends.
I want to know
how much to believe
so that after you have left me
and the real bond begins

after I have left you
the refusal will be in triumph
and not a loss.

II

I wanted to know
what was happening
then.
I ran to you
waving my arms
and cried

"The mountain is on fire,
the mountain is on fire,
who will stop
the mountain burning!"

But you weren't with me
you were away with
somebody else.
Your mouth was full of
her breast, heaving like scissors
on the outer edges of her skin.

You made me
alive with anger.
I went off
tramping down the river
and made
in the rocks
a bird—I gave it flesh
and a hideous name
and called it you,
sent it flying
where no one else could see
and brought it down
with another stone.
Then I lay on my back
in your blood
as the mountain burned
in the dust and the
wild strawberries
and you,
undisturbed by it all,
went on loving her
instead of coming with me
to watch it burn.

And you did love her,
right into the sand.

I saw you hesitate for a moment
on the brink of her thighs
but then
you drove her down
down and down
tearing your face
for her
on the cold hard sea
and your eyes bled
needing more than anyone could give.

I cried
as the mountain fell to ash
and from ash into stone
but I kept on burning
and being burned
until she divided us
with a final death
and drove you away from me
out of the tide
and into the hands
of the darkening trees.

III

I nearly missed you
altogether
this time—
I was stamping around my knees
in mud
and peered up
over the ledge
to your stone.
There were birds there, my love
and a music box that
sang if I wanted it to—
at first I thought it was
all quite nice
but then I discovered
the shredded bones of people
half-lost in feathers,
people I had hardly known.
I touched a hand and
pulled out the body
of a boy. Pieces of him
had already learned cruelty.
There was a dinner gong
and wind chimes for the wind,

an elaborate setting
for so many dead.

You must have turned quite mad
with the sun.
I thought you were
the prince of this place
but look at you now
watching me from
three forests away,
your eyes as slow and blind as thumbs.
I thought this was
your island,
this palace for the dumb.

You told me
this was your throne
so I came here
and found a tree instead
with branches so smooth
I had to dance all around.

But you can't abandon me here like this
and if you do
I shall decide my own way back.
I am tired of birds
and sick of dancing.
I am half-afraid of you.
The light I am fading with
is a graveyard for lovers—
everything ends here
alone with the cold.

IV

I was not sure
that I believed what he was doing
as he sat there at the window

all winter long with his flashlight
dragging things out of the water
and onto the sand.
He wanted
some relic of the past to reappear,
some wreck on a
visionary reef of gold,
a naked goddess,
the treasure he once made me
knowing I would lose it all.
In his torchlight
he made the birds go dancing,
he called down planes—
all winter long
it was like this,
he never changed.
Only once I dared to creep away
to be alone
and looking back I saw him
shine the light
at his own direction,
crumple his shaving mirror
and stuff a hundred shapeless pieces
down the eye of his horrible throat.
I came back
hoping he wouldn't notice
my broken hands. I cared for him
too well.

Then it was summer
and where he guided in the
ships at night
he shone a false beacon
and was the dangerous rock.
Slumped in his chair
he is bearded now,

he has never moved
but he likes the change.

I am his widow
lost to the autumn and the
spring. I lie alone
and nod to day and night
like kelp,
mistress of his harbour,
keeper of his silent chair.
When this day is over
there will be nothing left for me to do
so I sing in circles
and wade out through memories of his light
not for any lover's eyes.

V

He may come back alive
some time
someday soon
he may come walking
out of the nettles, his boots
astounded with sting,
his long face blistered
from the kiss of a sun-dried girl.

He is my hunter
too.
When we lie down in the trees
I close my eyes to love
but I am never asleep for long.
I am always
watching him, he is nobody's shelter
in any way.

Last time he went from me
too long

to somebody else's ruins
another continent away.
Children ran wild
through his beard, he was not
careful enough, he
didn't remember me.

Is there really this much
desolation
or is it just that
I've found it all?
—Who decides these things
you said
as I crept away
and threw a stone from my shoulder
over the sun.

Next time you leave for the forest
I will be staying here.

VI

Up until now
I felt as though I had been
forever hanging on to something.
I half-loved you,
the empty places took on the shapes
of change, the stone I felt
survived, still as stone
and I lived within you
where the wilderness invaded
destroying the equivalent of days.

But I had forgotten about the city.
Because I loved you
too much
I had marked time
on the spot of our solitude—

"Goodbye—
I will only be leaving for a year"
is now what I know I must say

but who am I fooling
wrapped in the coin of
snake skin, coiled in the
sight that crumbles in
expectation

I swear
I will never be back again.

O alphabet,
you letter-perfect
language! It is difficult
this—
coming down.
In a woman's law
there is no alternative
to sadness.
There is only blackout
beyond her
and no cure for what is
temporary
and lies between.

There you will remain,
angrily
at the memory of it all,
unable to penetrate
a similar heart as you own
you will try everything,
even to outlive me
with some amazing or immortal feat.
Finally, in exasperation
I will eat my way out
of my own skinny veins

and unwind in all the labour
of that cruel and last descent.

I will betray you, my lover,
I will ruin you.
I will smash my rotten detestable heart
on all the preoccupation
of your mind.
Not even wounded
I will lie accused for centuries
cold in the slime of the
snake seraph with his headdress
and fangs
vomiting up my memory
of you
broken with the murder
of the universe to come.

III

Yet I shall go into a bee
With mickle horror and dread of thee,
And flit to hive in the Devil's name
Ere that I be fetchèd hame.

Remembering a Man

Treading water
I followed the movement of the fish
upstream
and sent them
with a strange intractable claw
flowing north where the river pales
to meet your eyes.

A day before the sunrise
you set out, your face
as hard as chain and
already narrowed to the vision's end.
I awoke and noticed
bear tracks fresh across my thighs
but ruled you out,
my hunter who stays around
when the expectation is full of blood.

After you went away
I swear I discovered
places even farther away
from myself. The forest was black
but no darkness nearer
than I was to you.
Clouds gathered
at the gates of my ruined country,
it was harvest time.
High above me an eagle was circling,
slowly, slowly
bringing messages from the dead.

First Light

I moved down over the black road
remembering the way
that led between us,
feeling your dark absence
before me, as it should have been,
under the blood
that flowed out, abandoning your grave.

But you passed by me
almost recognizing
what I saw.

My eyes no longer accuse for themselves,
but this time I know you—
I know who you are.

And I have begun to dream
of pieces broken into things,
chips of bone dust
swirled in our shape
till my life has become
the breath of someone new.
Now the slain lie everywhere
on the forest leaves,
sharing between them
what we lost, though bones entwined
soon catch
the light of very nearly day.

The Executioner's Christmas

The dead are forecasting
bad weather.
When they called me
out of my sleep
I wanted to tell you
"They aren't really there"
but you had gone away again
after some other kill.

I drew myself
all around me. I couldn't escape
don't you see,
so don't ask me
to come with you anymore.
The dead
turn their eyes down,
their heartbeats lessen.

They might scream,
"IS THIS ALL!"
and I would have to tell them
—yes.

I followed you
down into the orchard
frightened because I heard their voices
and smelled the blood in the fire
as I drew too near.
I wanted you
whole
as you once were
but when I was finished
all I could find
was a knife, a few small bones

and you
with your black, black wings.

Passing Time

It was morning
and still the moon hung over us
a strand too heavy
for any lover's eye.
We lay alone
hand in hand
our bodies sorted out and
given names,
no particular flesh
but one shape that crumbles
into the shape of all dead things.

The mind may lay it out
and give it reasons. Often
it was blindness or whatever

first came into sight
that made me go on
staying here.
You turned
in the dim, unmade room
loving
the error of the day, your love—
a parting sore.
Half a world apart
without regret
we lay
and nowhere did my late mouth
open to cry.

Corcovado

I spread my arms for you
ninety-two feet across
in an evening park,
where the silhouette of
Jesus
stood smiling naked
from a hill.

I reached to touch
the yellow mist
for you
and dropped my sculptured mountain
as a hunchback
drops his weary shoulders
dancing to reveal
his painful struggle
more or less in vain.

Once More

We sit at the river
you, drunk already,
and I
your days feed.
Everything that I didn't want to know
about you
you told me in the first five minutes
we were alone.
After that
there was nothing more
worth mentioning.

You are almost
too grim. You are
only a madman
in all the spaces I can't fill.
Try singleness for a while.
Try forgetting about
the purpose of everything—
nothing *ever* happens;
diversity boils down to this.

Somehow
my body will survive.
Though not for long.
I toss you
random pieces from my thigh,
fingernail parings,
a section of hair.
I could last. What might vanish
is the offering I never made.

The Flight

You cannot leave me
    he told me
out on a cold mountain,
his lips shrill upon our troubled skin.
You cannot leave me
    —an old wound set in so far
        that it cannot mend—

The triumph is not in
the man himself, nor in the
women among him.
The triumph is the hazard of the man.

Sadness is a fixed thing
    I told him after
on a windy hill of skaters.
Ice flashed from behind his eyes,
there was a stone
    blinding him.

After the Battle

Unaware that anything was wrong
I crawled out from under you
after the battle
and stood
remote and changed
in the place beside you
that should have been your own.

Yours was the only corpse, I noticed.
Some small animal
circled cautiously behind your eyes.

Your mouth had no edges,
no place for hanging on.
It was, instead, a place for lizards.

Your body is the sanctuary
for all the wildlife
that isn't me. A remnant of your hand
encloses all.
I am some bad flower
sent deliberately to spoil your grave.
I grow best in blood.

Lying here,
you accuse me in the darkness
without even turning
certain beauty to design.
You want everything to reappear
out of a past I can't explain.

I am not at fault
because you fell in a place of stone.
The blood will dry,
the stone will still be cold.
Your body will be
the singular thing
containing all.
That is—
        nothing to remain,
        nothing to destroy.

Winter Poem
for Jeanne

Walking on the beach
glanced from a stone
        through lunch hours
                bookstores

blond hair on red winter,
tires frozen to the narrow road—

I cried in the snow
—steep side of the mountain—
freezing snow
—hurrying up the mountain's slope—

I am still the leafless girl
you fed to the snow
that dark winter,
the cold mystery
        now warmed over
        thawed for love.

But now the snow's run down
and the winter is empty as ever.
I wait by old rains
trapped in pink pools like fish
though my boundaries utter
their endless drift.

They All Came Tumbling After

Deceive, eyes,
patches of brain lie
like dance floors,
our minds prone
distractedly
in the arms of madness.

You refuse my eyes
        this time
from a loss of balance
moist with dancing

and I beg
for what the night
could be

I ask you
why the Trojan women
had glass nipples—;

when they dance
their navels speak of you.

IV

Yet I shall go into a mouse
And haste me unto the miller's house,
There in the corn to have good game
Ere that I be fetchèd hame.

The Magician's Fist

I am the magician:
there are some new children playing
in the magician's fist.
They teach me
to be unaware of guns,
that I don't need magic
to make believe.

I walk in the sand
like a man would wade through syrup
dropping some spell at every glance
understanding little
of what I do.

I will make you, the prince,
surrender to my city,

submit to my occupation
(temporarily).
My bed is the prison,
but for you, as well,
it will be a grave.

(In the end
the magician tightens his grip
and altogether
disappears. The city is the space
left vacant by his mind, the prince
welcomes some other princess
and age creeps upon him,
unsuspecting,
like a snowstorm
with only some clouds and rivers
to herald its approach.)

Tiger

The hand that fell upon me
was the music of a dancing tiger—
as it took upon my arm I
heard the river of something I meant for love.
There in the grass I lay outside my action,
I envied the birds, the eyes
they could eat from my head—
for a little waiting
they could have my dancing master and the guilt
that bore beside him
till he dared to choose the will
that was given to me to do.

My tiger learned to dream, too.
When I laid my face in the river
to cool my tears
a rat swam under my eyes

and came swimming
into a thousand dreams I
screamed from. Rat? Tiger?
I forget now which was which.

But that dancing master, alone in his evil ways
between the pages of wig and ruffle—
which of my acts was done to me
so in secret that I wake here
seeing him teaching the children songs and kisses
to one side of all tigers in my arms.

January 6

Since you left
I have waited like the hours
unseen and heavy

and although you have been
gone for less than
a week

it has rained every day but
it was good for the garden
anyway;

the window above the sink still rattles
—I don't remember why—
I bought some new filters
to clean the furnace.

The long days mate with
the nude on the calendar.

I have packed time like a suitcase.

Now there is nothing left to do
but organize my boredom.

The House and the Garden

These days are treacherous—
like cut vines and murderous roots
the flowers in the garden
grow deliberately out of proportion.
Insensitive, they are colourless
and don't leave any room for the grass.

Trees uproot themselves
sending hidden fingers
to hide the sun.

The stones are automatically bored.

When I walk outside
devils sit and guard the rabbit holes.
The fence is indifferent
and the vegetables never get
enthusiastic about anything.

I've given up simply trying
to understand. Small animals mate
between the walls of my house.
I'm afraid it too will soon
disappear—most of my neighbours
wish I would leave.

Because of them
there hasn't been any weather
for over a year.

I am such a sad young girl
and they are such horrible old men.

Celebration

Being somebody's last woman
and the only passenger of the day
I rode out after madness,
that long journey beginning nowhere
meeting shyly at motels
not for each night's love,
but sliding around the edges
from earth to earth
on parts of a face
that love wore out.

Of course I'm still living.
No one has taken too much blood
although I admit I stole some extra
where fine needles had coffered
bundles and rolls of it. I came back
after to burn the hospital down.

But no one will find me here
asleep in my bones as polished as the night.
I am bled now
like the end of a spear
and blunt as a carpet
ruined once by careful feet.

One day the right disguise
will work, the right frame
slide into place
like counted medicine.
One day I may give up everything
and wear that disguise
to its final sleep.

Time Around Scars

Going back the last time
propped up on the bleeding walls
a broken-down car and
stealing a razor from
a slivered man who
wailed about this the
last time it happened—

I thought
—I'll send him an ambulance
   full of blood

   or at the trigger moment
   think of something else...

I came back to you again
only the day after

but the unhappened moment
is real blood.

Mirror

I walked into your mirror
not remembering that I was blind
On the other side
I found all the people
who had ever looked at themselves,
people with one side silvered
who not only could see each other
but also the reflection
of everything else.
Having me at last
a tear slid between your eye

and the glass
and I slipped out
where all water goes—
a usual way.

Refusal

These are not all lovers,
these half-shapes.
When they reach for each other
their teeth leave marks,
they spend
in each other's blood
something beyond love.

They are insects,
and what is worse
they are insects that feed upon
their own decay.
They have pursed reality
from some
worn-out maggot hell
and there is
no saving them,
there is
no yesterday
when they come down.

One day, all suddenly over,
they find themselves alone. The rocks,
for a change,
have worn down the waves.
There is
danger in sanity
there is danger
in sanity
there is danger
in not understanding loss.

V

Swithold footed thrice the wold,
He met the Night-Mare and her nine-fold,
Bid her alight and her troth plight,
And aroynt thee, witch, aroynt thee!

Exposure

My ribs are torn
like old whore petticoats.
I have pictured
sly unmiraculous women
hiding their faces in shawls
of long bodies, being very
old and inaccessible—
trembling old ladies with
their canes, ahead on the last
trip of their lives.

I turn in a green
and yellow globule flowing
endless as a nighthawk's
spread of wings; very small babies
have very small cries—
I scream and yet
no one hears me.

I am like a mole
crawling through the earth. I must go
around the stones. Why is it
that I'm tired of talking to
myself? I want *everyone* to know.
How can I say that this is really
quite serious without upsetting
the magnificent mantelpiece

and chipping the fragile china bodies
beyond all recognition?

I'm tired of all these drunken poets
with their five-mile-an-hour slide rules
surveying the city's mainline vein.
I want to try all over again, begin
by saying—every chance I get
I'm going to hide in the basement
and count the cracks on the ceiling.
I refuse to give up my obsesssion.

Kinetic creations are taking on
my personality—I am not for
anything, not even myself. It seems
that the bold pavilion of the world
is only the surface serenity
of an inner anxious city.
The city is in my mind,
I go there to take off all my clothes,
to iron all the grandmothers
flat out straight and to play
practical jokes, to never get
laid—you're *all* too much for me.
I want to buy anything I want to
with my face but Russia won't
join in. Russia's power-hungry. And I'm
responsible for all that goes on
here. I have to protect myself.

Money is the *only* kind of profit.
The word God brings on laughter
but the sign of the dollar
stretches far out into space. I want to
know everything that is going on;
why can't I buy freedom for $3,500 a piece?
Why can't I leave the salt mines
in Siberia? I want to burn the
bureaucracies but I won't.

You test me every day. I won't be
ready until all the world is ready; I
want to see it all at once.
I'm tired of building jigsaw puzzles.
I keep losing pieces of the sky.

I run in patchwork traffic
circles. I am forever on a corner
waving on the flow of
transcontinental buses and tin
horse chariots. Someday
we will meet in Warsaw.

I resolve to give up everything.
I say that the real thing is happening
and that you are there—
that you are real. "To be free
means free to choose whose
slave you want to be;
—slaves of no special colour
    and the links of chain
    fall into no special order;
    how good an actor do you
    have to be
    and play God?"—

My mind is a speck of sound
within a silent universe. I hear
people swallowing lies,
vomiting self-satisfaction; I watch
my ideas become misused. I am
undulating near your body
like an army several thousand dollars
high. I will try not to try
any harder next time.

I am dressed in souvenirs
of abortion—trouble with the

voices, colour, design and sound,
they are breaking to destroy
my dreams as I, in cosmic laughter,
represent the human race by
being sick on Sunday morning
and talking about the president.
Do you remember the store-manager
martyrs, the importance of
sufficiency, the sunken continents
inside your brain?

Black hoods in the red
square are causing a
landslide for peace. I become
the sniper of the world, my mouth
devours the public sidewalks and I have
stolen all your wives from where you
chained them. The interior of my
stomach *needs* something. My psychoanalyst
things I'm perfectly all right.

It's my way of talking to the world
when I say I wear a wig of blood and my
eyes are as hollow as your cerebral passage;
it's my way of letting you know that
the streets are running from under
my feet and wherever I go there's
someone groaning into a bloody
toilet. I wish you had
to paint me in the nude. I believe
I have something to contribute.

I posed for a newspaper clipping of
myself standing sideways on the sun
never realizing the potential power of the
twenty-five million institutions who
sought my name—how eager they are for blood,
how sexless they are for

being condemned on neither one side
nor the other. When they
wake up they'll have to start all over.
Paris is full so we still
import these foreign doctors.
(Skillfully I manipulated
my character for them like a piece
of chess across a jigsaw setting
of rotting platforms and penthouse stairs.)

I have lived too long in a thick
black shoe like a foot, I have stepped
through too many days and uncovered my
face on too many coins. I want to
retire from life to the supermarkets
and cultivate a habit of shifting myself
into dragons and turning the blade
from my face to drawing intellectually
perverted pictures of snot-nosed
rabbis. And careening across America
asleep to the sweet white rocks
of Alcatraz. I want to dump the Editors
of Reality like a chip of sawdust and
bury their smatterings somewhere
on a San Francisco hill.

I will scream with joy someday when
my motionless world leaves its continuum
orbit and becomes a neon lampost absurd
and laughing in a roaring winter night.
We are both lonely, scanning the skyline
of the moon, jumping off onto the
Empire State—suddenly I want to drink turpentine
or call you long-distance in Sacramento.
Whispering my memories won't make you
reappear, you are a burned cigarette
hole left on an eyelash in the rain.

Undressing to the sirens of a Los Angeles
night I am the crime of dead intoxication,
counting numbers, dreaming symbols—
my skeleton face, you say, is the ash
of poetry, that I am too far away and
my shadow has hardened into stone.

I have given up three times unsuccessfully
and been shifted
in and out of dreams like the
opium alleys in the downtown night.
I demand a sanity trial, I want you
all there to witness my one
symbolic disguise.
Yes I am resting briefly in catatonia,
campaigning the Creativity of Nothing—
it may be the simplest resolution
I've ever decided to make.

Entrance of the Celebrant
1972

I

Gathering in the Host's Wood

i

They were gathering there
in the host's wood,
breaking fire and filling the
night with news.

To the owl's glen crept
the hunted, covering themselves
with leaves in the dawn settling
over them.

Skuld, the Elf-Queen
parting in the dark,
trailing a small guilt, picked
blood from her hair.

My small friend—I thought
he had left me. Pagan,
his love dripping out of me,
rising on the riverbank
before the feast.

ii

The Queen's heart is a step
to madness. My tongue kisses
the cold kiss of her
mouth, her lips
the borders of constellations.

I turn aside.

Down in the dimly lit passage
a simple light burns. It is

the Queen's heart returning
to her cold breast.

      iii

Skuld's forest is where the
dead go, silently
between the leaves. We must be careful
not to wake them, treading
frozen foot over
fish eyes picked clean
by birds.

Cold fog
and the hammers of death. Skuld
willing her cold way into
everything. She
as a toad, and I a squirrel,
embrace in the
royal fire, spitting ash
in memory of a king.

Birthstone

Trapped by stars that see
is any sister, star or stone,
reaching the green rocks with
tidal wand, her wounds time-still.

In the night's past time
I am red rock cut in the vulture's eye.
In him my hands thrust down
the throat; I wish;
I breathe; I wish
my hands caught waves on the
broken eye or shore.

Once more time-trapped by
that sea, I am sister
to stone; for who is lost
hastens the dumb tongue to hate
the stone whose sister speaks of loss,
                    stone of denial.

                    November 16, 1969
                    Metchosin

Anserra

Nine times her curse
through nine seasons
entered me, in the
dark roots of hollows
awaiting the damp marsh call.
Who can know
where the hag nests
and in what madness?
Cold and wild, my memory,
crouched in the earth's loss,
listening in the reeds.

Would he come, then—
will he—
ever?
        Within my skull
the black night cowered, its fear
descends, trusts to a world's shame.

She told me,
"A child dies—deceives us
into sadness.
        Love's curse is no one's
mercy—like the child.

The living enter in
one invisible seed. Death chooses
the kiss of the widow,
a life alone."

Sadness upon sorrow
is how the hours
enter me; darkness on the
water and wind
at the water's edge.
                         Sorrow upon sorrow
a cold seed gives birth
remembering nothing. Death resembles it—I know
well.

          It is not
deliverance—I believe in the
life we die into. Sleeping and
dreaming how I would
love him if I knew him
or wake
from time to time
and grow
alone.

Acelin's Burial

The arrow falls
and these wounds enter the child
asleep. No sounds remember
but they echo into stone; no journey follows
but the half-asleep awakening her to fear.

She is helpless in the
deep wood
only her heartbeat enters now.
She dreams of the black bolt

tearing her, of blood in her
wet veins
thickening to earth.

Then hunger comes. On the
third day she crawls
from the empty womb, fleshless
out of darkness and falling
toward birth. Death makes
feathers on the same day, scatters
his seed. All bound by
feathers in the
black wood—death conceives it
and she is a bird.

No one breathes
in the lichen
forest, leaf-buried in a grave
the dark moon chose. Prowling
to the lip's edge fastened by
tears, shadows cross her
torn face and she is
gentler now.

Facing Moons

This night spent
watchful, waking,
no sound as the
moment of all sound
echoes
anything else,

this moment facing moons in
darkness, dull glow
from watchers, here and I

here but not here
before myself
inside—
moon of sleep constant inside
sleep, moon that I am
creeping down.

The Herd

No one would come here;
to this place light is cold and
water is too deep for swimmers.
No one yet has been able to find me
nor would enter willingly these spaces, clear
and dark where I, like roots, find
upward from the edges that I am somewhere
nearer myself.
The darkness moves, not around
but into me. I might be here
forever, one moment might
hold me to the ground or shake me
from becoming anything else.

All I am becoming anyway
is wrong. I can hear the water
though cannot remember the sounds—
one music is all things disappearing
and the face raised slowly
is fathering the body of a man.

Again and again I grow
no older—it is this face that comes out
to recognize itself, hiding somewhere
maybe behind his heart. The words tell
again and *again* and maybe *this* time
dream of finding what it was they say.

I am here, would rather remain,
when all others die,
the caged shadow that is the first to live.
I could not betray it, what is mine
to hate, nor allow ruin and hatred together.
They alone might dream of waking to be wanted,
strayed out for the moment
they could not stop to pretend.

I thought of sleep and her
cold ways but had no memory and so
kept sleeping. Now I cannot stop it happening
but grow alone and live as anyone,
careless of distances
and haunting the dark ground.

Crow Wood

I do not know
the shape of that man,
hunched under the
tree's bank pocked and shady
to the river's edge.
He sinks into the nettle's touch
and all thorn knows his grip.
At such times the moon
is a birthmark on his face.

When light fails I know
he is asleep in there—
I would not go on
that way. His wood is the
echoing one and every man
his ghost.

I had not guessed
I would know him

if he came—small under the
root's drip where earth clings heavy
to sleep. I had not guessed
his shadow would
fall this way or who would enter
the dark shapes first.

Already his heart
is quickening to heat; he will
awaken soon. I turn
in the cramped seed
opening on his hand, rooting for memories
never mine to know.
I had not waited
for lies to become familiar
while crows in the old wood
were calling to be born.

I saw him pass. I think the moon
had risen behind his eyes
and night was a
carrying tide.
He went with water
to earth under the
crow's nest
and there only his white face
troubles them now.

They do not sleep.
Sometimes they see him in those
close fields they watch,
circling into the high shadows
of his last descent.

The Blind Mapmaker
for Phil Heron

The few edges reached
from open places
in his hand
are places at night where
the animals go to eat,
or, finding him there
perform a small ritual
that joins him to the dark. He casts
their bones as a shield
before him,
flaps his dry wings and
vanishes up inside.

So he spread like thorn
to take the cold
from a winter's eye. He never stopped
or reached
the impassable point. It was his
purpose to go beyond
all danger
into what mouths could feed him
or be fed alone.

Things were tightening.
Every year stretched within him
to carve the man outside.
He saw the mountains
rise and fill up the
valleys, and then go
as later, sprung from water,
he joined the valley at the
river's end.

He held his death forming
in the cleft of a palm, fingers

turned open to the grip below
and a black pelt shadowing
the anger of a frozen man.
He began to know the earth
as other to himself, dripping cold
and naked he feared for the absence
of anything more.
Sleep took him in, he sensed himself
with difficulty. It was contained
inside him, within his arms.

There are no more secrets
now, the cold has
eaten everything. A thin face turns
sideways, defying the dark. Still
it returns, where at the centre of
himself he comes to the edges,
one at a time, unsure
of what is there
to hinge the blind memory
and the darkness he has become.

Night-Hawk

All night the
deep bird inside me
circles the
gripped skin. At times in the
cold light
he edges fire.

Beyond him there is
darkness. We know
the mark. Bird of
the bone of which
we are naked, bird of the
black flesh
driven into night.

He comes out of
nowhere, invisible as
loss. Dry as a shadow
his old seed split
from a corpse's heart.

He is black
inside me
circling into life.
I remember that
one night
when all, when everywhere
memory fails.

There is still time. Our
fingers loosen the earth.
Sinking back
into the
green fold, out of the
earth's lock
tightening still.

I was falling
even then. That world
edges this wound, that bird
did not choose.

He was
part of us. He fed
in the
moth light and now
you sleep.

He is part of us.

Now I remember
a dark stone

where you were
sleeping

trailing blood,
trailing blood.

II

To Someone Asleep

All night long I
covered you with
leaves. Dry as the
morning you
smelled of bones.

Small birds crept
under your
shadows, in secret
that is shadow, in the flowers
that are blood.

Where is the
way in, where
is the way? Tap on my
blind window,
rustle the wind.

When I whisper
it will be
entering you.
Your ear is a cave
where animals go to die.

I am a
ghost moth
crawling on your
belly, I am
fungus to your
thighs.

Eared owl, feared
owl
this is the dark
I hunt.

Dog Star
for W. S. Merwin

I do not remember
the night; that night
I had no way with him.

I was the dog child
follower of stars.
I was the dark one's
brindled stray.

That night the night
entered him—
I left him there.
Uphill where the hawk lives
I carried his bones to earth.

> *Dog child* he whispered,
> he was nearest to me then.
> I came and the wind
> covered us—we lay alone
> in sleep.

But rising out of that
dark hill, the shadow

of our last flight fell,
not caring
how the stars shone or
knowing the dust of that
final light.

This was the first night
dream I remember:
two wreaths of the
old gods
were fire and blood.
That was the last time
I followed him again.

Dog child he called me,
I turned to leave.
Stars hung
like chains on my sleep,
moonlight
barred the way.

"The Night, the Real Night..."

I had dreamed him before,
the stranger within me
I have been waking beside. For a long time
it was so dark
I couldn't remember anyone.
Then I wanted it to be night again.

You said this
today—
I understood you then. I was
confused; you said
"I have vanished!"
But somehow I remembered

after all—*that* sadness
I was waiting for.

I can see him again, walking
into the blind sun
so almost now if I wake
everything frightens me.

I am cold, it is all so
strange to me; how could I deceive,
not knowing you a minute longer,
this gladness we have shared
together in our first loneliness.

Finding Love

The thin smoke stings my eyes;
my fingers, like bees, in search of you.
It is doubtful, coming here by night,
that I shall return by you
in the same shape as I came.
We look alike, sometimes
lying side by side, love's own posture
but all an empty stake.

I waver like a child
having fled the sea. It is not
what I expected, the dark fires,
the sullen turn of ground. Everything must learn
How *I* have dreamed it:
a misshapen thought, or else,
a darkness forever without a name.

From my bed I could hear
the ripe wound open, the thick sea
pouring in. I told you, then,
the first lie I had in my heart;
the carcass of a dull animal
slipped between our sights.

Wake

The ghost of an old moon
promising nothing
bends where the mountains rise up
echoing defeat.
Love, there is no greater love
between us—
such dark honour
has little to deceive.

For can I deny him
who made this love
and now would have it breaking?
This fear is coming into me; I waver
but cannot
hold out to him.

    Wake, love,
he tells me,
to face the lonelier sleep.
Am I dying? Am I
always dying?
    Listen, love,
he whispers, as each breath scorns
the wakeful call.

Disparates

There in her black skirt hides
the skin of a deer,
the flesh under the shape pulled taut
to hide no other reason
than her own.

I am this shape
               of *this* woman or

these five women tugging at rags
tossing the twisted
animal skin inside them,
pulling me always from the centre
out.

I am this shape of this animal
the skin does not change
but is tossed in the shape of a man.

                                   These five women
retrieve him, let loose their skin
set aside their skirts

and the man crawls in among them
as anybody else's death.

He arrives just the same
from the wrong direction. Reduction,
a funeral style, the man says, smiling
as the skin burns away in confusion.

Their small lives
are his idea
also.

Sounding

    She
in an attitude of faces,
spent what the just gave back
and kept on taking.
                         I was becoming
more than certain.
                    It is the way
the finger closes
over whatever it is she holds,
a force that hides her from

what is hidden—things I should
remember more carefully, the
closed thought open to delivery.

That she is around me
in every form whose shape she cannot
contain, I am becoming
more than certain. She is
the same as I am and
I am the same
as anyone alone.

But the blank walls are all
turning eastward
where I have crept along
and offered myself the end.
      It is she
who risks the last
for a final call,
not to this face but
another where her own might change.
      She follows me
                        attentive
      to the failing edge.

Glaistig

> *Growth like the fern to them,*
> *Wasting like the rushes to them,*
> *And unlasting as the mist of the hill.*

Down in the earth's memory
damp caves of insects are
swarming for
food.

In the dry belly
for centuries
feeds a dark incurable sore.

Her memory is a stone
falling into
water. Her skin has a
fish's touch,
honoured by toad,
by creatures of the marsh.

In the throat, in the
souring limbs
all heat is
the heart. Her eyes
on the river are
straining to remember:

There are small fish
silver and secret.
She fills her beak with
their blood.

The Tribe of the Sea

The old men were watching
far before the moon
came out—they knew her eyes
were the moon's colour.

Into her arms she
had them, held on
half a century. Flowers blew
in the waste of her
reason: in her body
they found a grave; in her kiss,
seclusion.

The tide could uncover
every trace of her, leave them
stranded on the vanishing
shore. Dark fingers squeezing
old love out of them—they expect
completion but she is
naked with the new moon's life.

The dark weight of a
night's haul within them,
the old men turned east and cast
to an offered shore. Trailed
from her thin grey wake
into morning, she was riding
the last wave out.

Night and Fog

These are the black woods, my
first asylum. Down at the
river's edge, in my own way
given to the monstrous.

Voices I called to
out of the blind fog
drew me that way.
Into the wet woods
calling them: they do not
answer and I am
possessed again.

> "Stay with me—you who are
> other to all
> I am—you whose darkness is the
> shadow of my birth."

I could not escape it—
they were
everything. Moss grew
over their faces, seaweed
was their hair.
Theirs was the way the
wet sounds as
everything condenses. Theirs were
the still fires, the moon's frail
worth.

> "Stay beside me—you I have
> returned to
> more times ever than
> before; you I have returned to
> other than anyone,
> other to myself."

I shiver. It edges
the unfamiliar; it
lessens me. Dark with the secret I am
hunted under, theirs are the wounds
beneath the scar.

Voices out of the night
and the fog, voices of the womb
conceiving me. I believe in
creation, of flesh that binds
and is mine without knowledge.

I had forgotten more: I have
lost more than remembrance.
While I slept
the voices were dying—
they are dead now and
do not answer.

> "Stay with me. I need your
> comfort now. One wish is that

you would return and
all would be warm again."

Stay with me. Out on the
trailing edges of darkness
I scatter their last bones before me
to my will.

III

The Opened Grave

Promises to the dying are easy!...
Now I have slept, and am awake;
I am dead and live indeed!

I. THE DREAM OF SLEEPING

The dead come in the evening
bringing their messages gathered into
dreams. I saw no one who escaped it,
but few remembered—death trapped them
into magic, not by dreams.

The way to return by, closes.
Sometimes a dream went away, I was
halfway there. Then a dream came
and I was at last awake.

I have no memory of seasons,
the cold fingers that touched on my face
before seasons came. I would have
drowned or burned holes in my body,
glad of a reason to feel decay.

In the cold of the morning
my narrow fingers
rattle their bones.
I am someone
dead for a long time.

II. THE DREAM OF WAKING

The end was unclouded—
I remember swimming up from
the darkest part of the night
through years that curled frowns on my features,
past anything that had never been.

Beyond me in the forest
a grave was speaking. A skull whispered
warnings though my feet entered first.
The day became a dream I woke from,
waiting till darkness became my face.

I remember the beginning
like the first day of the world.
I floated like a scar along some river
listening for an answer
whenever I called. This dream,
on the edge of things, troubled me—
the dream I was lost and halfway there.

In the morning I woke up
under the forest.
I broke my wings, I slipped away.

III. THE DREAM OF DYING

The dead dream of dying, too—
they come in bells, wear
ragged horns. Always
I find them breathing

though my fingers trace the dead man
to their bones. I would

break this sleep, my last sleep,
to find them hanging, sharp hooves down
among the dull stone.

For What We Were

For less of what I am
I could deny him more—
things that are not my own
but other, only to themselves.

And the new moon—
did we not dream her, the first night
from a cold strained bed,
and trace her final circle down the sky
to sleep for all the worn month's care?

I believe in this dreading, finally
there were signs. Death held his
dark call unanswered—
for this love we made
in madness we were cast.

Turning Back
for Haidée Virgo

When things end, I think
—*I knew it would*—
each lance reversed in the wound
as time gave well. But it is
always the same.

I don't ever know.
No, I do not remember,
is it what ends or
what never began? I turn
where I should have stopped turning. Reluctance
changes things.

Each night I want to
bring the turning to a close,
say "dance, I am
dying to death," say "sleep
I am warm," my sleeping
being lonely, my dreams mistaken
among the stones.

So like a bird
she does not see.
Being small regrets something—
so soft like a girl
death happens that way.

I left myself, ended
said, end. It was
not perfect, I turned upon
a face full my own, breathed
myself. I am captured
I said—she didn't care.
She was a boy and had a man's kiss.
When my hand went over her heart
it was a final hand. Look,
she said, turned back to the beach
for the snail who was not my child.

Fire-Feast

That night flew in
as the shape of a bird;

to the foxhole, little friend,
I ran my course.

A warm secret we knew
was comfort then: the quickening
of the year meant danger.

The first month you
stayed beside me, then with
less care for
gentleness now without wounds.
Under the cold slopes
our blood crept for
safety; in the thickets
they hunted for slaughter.

Then you were a ghost
to me, little and
ruined when you broke from the
moon's heat and ran to earth
in the lost light.
                    They made fire
to your madness and
drew you out, careless of the
wood's green for all that death
soon won.

            Don't betray me. Bloodless
the thorn will survive where they
danced for nine lives
on the ashes of the feast
but fallen and unmated I will have
no one. To the fire's edge
I trusted them but now I follow
my own footprints back.

            Crouched in the
dull passage I remember how

I saw you, already running
far in the unfamiliar dark.

Simply:

the road, the flaw
descending to the
crossroads where the dead
think in stone their dreams
of flesh, but are careful
not to touch. Then—
I am there, I am

moving,   not yet
              not alive

but instant and fading
in dreams of skin
that turn to careful thoughts of stone.

Spoils

> *Weird woman that washest the garments,*
> *Make for us the self-same prophecy:*
> *Will any one of them fall by us,*
> *Or shall we all go to nothingness?*

There is news now
of a survival. Then she sits
and casts an old misfortune: too many
have survived while nobody lived
to think of more.

The numbers are slight, let us
recount the losses. We have nothing to fear,

a time in a space is small. "Listen love,
there are few of us." "Two of you,"
she whispers, and I in the dark
growing more or less alone.

Old woman
I think you are mistaken. Remember—
I have come here waiting for him.
"Love by him once,
though once taken, love's
too many." And these deaths I shall
mourn for him, whose body shall find no death
a bitter thing.

But once more let us lie together
where no one slain can hear us speak.
Reach for me his body
where the black crow dies
and white flowers pass
out of a ghost's land. There I might
know him still or I should go falsely—
carrying the cold news,
taking the dark way home.

The Kingfish Angel

Where blood melted under the river
the drippings fastened
to her eye below—
she hung on a skull
that other waters caught,
lured a man from his dogs
and they can't find pieces of him
anywhere.

She scattered the darkness in a
hail of bones; from this light

and not any other
he went missing.
Alone to the pond's end he came
as the water turned with news of the place
where the last of her lover waited to be burned.

But below the water
the surface was too still to see.
She watched for the boned man
whose face she can't remember—
one eye shifted the weight of the river
and piece by piece she carried him down.
The man dropped his fingers
out behind him, the blood drifted easily
over his scars.
And hanging there
under a sky ringing clear and hard—
looking down for a last time he had
no reflection, his face
inverted or any other way.

Death by Hanging

What I fear is no more than an end
to this—to lie unfeeling
        frozen—
        death by fire, by water
        death by hanging.

Yesterday I drowned
today I breathed water—
swam down furious
to fire through water,
dreamed the dream of
drowners

        so cold
just being there.

Alive Things and Dead

Always underfoot where the
grave shudders
have I found a place:
    Ice under the skin
    buried without covering—
    wound that is secret
    beneath the scar.

The dead stir
in each bone whispering
of old love,
in each sound
straining to remember. *Time is age and*
you are ending. I do not live
to want anyone.

Drawn as the white flame to
fasten the dry moth,
the damp closes in.
Touching water it is
drawn again, failed
as the body of an insect,
helpless
in the lessening weave.

Time is old and
you were ended. I did not live
to remember anyone.
Only underneath what the
grass shadows
have I found a way:
    To carry you with me
    everywhere
    in one thought deeper
    than the flesh could wish.

As Death Does

All these white flowers
darkened my sleep,
after you were gone and
after you.

All these grey insects
entered my dreams,
ticked back to me
and remembered.

Rub this
strange heat
out of my body, rub me
everywhere away.
Tangle me with
waterbugs, with
earthmould and
rain.

I share you with beetles,
I share you in my bones.
Bite into me and
open your mind to blood.

Turn to me now as
death does and
turn in me again. Squeeze your
strange heat
into my body, press me everywhere
under your skin.

I share you in darkness,
I share you with the sun.

Go on forgetting as
death does, as
death does even among bones.

Entrance of the Celebrant

If you could see me,
where I am and where
the forest grows thick and into me;
if you cold reach
the darkest centre of myself
and still know the sign of the animal
where it lies apart inside your skin—

then I would say,
that kiss is *my* kiss;
where your lips have touched
were others, and mine are still.

No one forgets
the music of the animal. I've heard
the sound of the old skin cracking
where this heart has become
the heart of something new.
                              If he could see me,
know me, and not forget it was
he who saw me

and that circles tighten and everything
narrows

but that even I am nearing completion,
that everything I have become is something
already gone—

then the dark trees, the sounds
of water across water, of blood
drying still over water—

then his music is the sound of
nobody listening; the animal I carve out
is the shape of darkness, a sound
that nowhere would dare to form.

Animal! Animal!
You are nobody! You cannot be
anyone.

But I had known that
long before your birth.

So you died then? Only the dead
can know. My lips revealed you
and my heart has eaten the hole.
Black fingers pulled a small black night
from between us. Animal, animal
so small are we

that no one wanting
deserved death more.

Grave-Dirt and
Selected Strawberries
1973

I. Grave-Dirt

for Seán

Genesis

He could not rest
until there was water,
finding his words hard—
blue nuggets at the
lip's edge.

He dreamed of water.
Once a drop fell
in the bare light
and the fire eased.
He licked it up.

Scrawling across his belly,
a tense yellow blank,
he woke up finding the earth
dry, covered with small dead
frogs.

Witchery Way

Sometimes an old man
crouches at the river—
sometimes he is someone
whose bones are not formed.

Sometimes an old woman
with fisher-skin quiver,
sometimes on the low bank
is hungry after blood.

First Man wrenched a
forked tree, spit
the bone. First Woman
was a warm pelt
to carry him into the ground.

"People don't tell out
about these things;
they keep them
down here in the body."
Be careful
of the wolf's cry—he knows
those ways well. Open
the toad's belly and you will
find him there.

"The bone at the back
of the head is best,
a tongue black and swollen
from skin whorls picked
at night." First Woman
was a night cat
prowling the red ant hills.
First Man was
victim, sometimes
a grey fox.

Sometimes an old man
whispers down the smoke hole,
sometimes an old woman
furrows in the wind.
My skin is thick
with the dark seed
of their coming—
the blade of a fine axe
wedged between my eyes.

In Memoriam

Lorne Smith, killed in a logging accident
Queen Charlotte Islands
Fall 1972

The stones
witness all death
knowing no comparisons.
They break
the stilled bone, haunt
the deep earth like a lair.

You are out there
brought down in
ignorance for all your
failings.
Men
for the wrong reasons
will remember you,
who dragged life to those
edges and pushed it over
one by one.

You did not answer
when that echo called,
as if your fate had warned you
preparing its own
comfort...

You turned your way.

Now from this sleep
the night rises—
the earth stands
awkward with your loss.

> Each stone marks your journey
out into the dark—
the trees not even knowing
your last forgiveness.

Because

An odd man
hollow-lipped and,
they say,
whose bowels fell
out
altogether
one winter

lives alone
and always has
because
loneliness in a
grey coat
is more welcome than a
guest in scarlet.

The Hermit

i

Agriv called to the
ravens—
Agriv, an old
man.

The ravens came for his
eyes; Agriv said
nothing.

Night passed and Agriv
saw the wind.

He shivered like a
blind man
eating alone.

ii

Agriv woke up
drowning

eels risked his
left nostril

creation was a
rock crab
spawning his
hooked ear.

Agriv breathed
in the thin light.

He called to the
East Wind.

Agriv heard
the crack of his
old skin turning

spoils of his
own waste

burn
for the sake of burning.

iii

Each hour
the ice shivered.
Agriv watched
a woman's face,
saw that the mirror
contained poison.

Shadows crossed his
mouth like
weird bones of the dead.
Agriv watched age
destroy the glass.

Water was calm.
Glass was silence.

Water held her
wet tears—
Agriv learned:

no woman's face
would ease him now.

iv

Agriv has eyes
like burned-out
stumps in a
second-growth
wilderness
where nothing will survive.

A gorged
complacent look

like too many
people
talking about their
lives.

v

For years he had lived—
a chip in his own
wound

not speaking
when lies were
forgotten

not pitying age.

His memory was
dust, layers
beneath his face

A man could be lonelier
always
sharing the same bed.

Grave-Dirt

One god
distributes the light.
By error on that day
he descends to hell.

Hell is just an impression

luck-balls from the
death-owl's mask.

Raven unsheathes his
beak-knife,
his voice is made of
glass.

Woodpecker is the
hero,
his bad luck is
crossed.

His words are
the colour of mutiny

mumbling about birth
in different dialects

never seen on Fridays
because on that day
he returns to hell.

A clerical error
a conjurer
a death.

Woodpecker is
turned upon
picking among bones:

the eagles, the
long songs,
are bad for the memory.

The Changeling

It all began
this way.
I came out

hatched by the warmth of my skin,
a blameless child
unprepared to enter in
where all the others go.

There were times
I was glad to remain unknown. I asked
for no name at all,
I was
nobody's accident
and could not prevent
what already had occurred.
So
they left me
and left me
and now cannot forgive me
for telling them
I am ready to go.

The Child-Bride

After a while I shall learn
that disappointment seizes
the worst of all my gains—
anything else becomes
a better prospect. It is quite insulting
to be vague and full of love—
as if I couldn't live
without him. Pride is loose
in my blood and then sets in.
One by one
I take all my things away,
wincing on the dark shelf
above the bridegroom
offering peace.

A casual ceremony, no
black goodbyes—no children

begging in the shadows toward alarm. Where?
How? As usual
I am caught
off guard.

This that has crumbled,
this is what I had.
I burned out in expectation,
night fell
earlier, a quick new life
or else, a clear one.
Nothing in between. I couldn't
allow it, not for anybody's sake.
I fell
and scraped my knees
badly—why was I there?
Food for my lover's
child-bride. Sullen stain.
And dead sounds,
the reverence of leaving.
Anywhere around
he'd shed me, what is it
that he wants so hard?
Earth alone is indestructible.
I lie in defeat for the years.

One-Sided Woman

i

Her heart is a bone
laced by the
moon's pull

For seven days
and seven nights
she is
his hunger

On one hand
she wears a ring,
in the other she
holds a knife.
Her tongue understands
no language
her face is
not beautiful.

ii

She knew by
drowning
she could not avoid the
past—

water filled her
silence
like an old scar
hoarding its own
depth.

iii

Between her legs is
the slash of an
underworld

bracken lips unfurling
shy to the
moss-folds.

One hopes
she is gentle
to rhythms of the
sea.

iv

The flowers she picked
and brought to him
died before she
got there:

her face like a
gargoyle on a
picnic
breaking open
more eggs
than were ever meant
to be eaten.

v

For five months
she paced the winter,
dark with
advancing power

Her breasts
hung like greed
to the shell of her
heat

Her eyes saw
out of habit

Her body outgrowing
its own sorrow.

vi

The person inside her
is beating the
damp walls—

knocking on stone
now and again
in the wreckage of
her dreams.

She is
wild-bitten and her
skull rattles.
She does not want to play
like other children.

      vii

She is tired
of weedy places
of thin voices in a
house with too many
rooms.

She imagines a
journey
out to the islands—
trailing a vague
hand,
floating
for the shark's sake.

      viii

She knows
the moth's oblivion
in a dry month.

She reads maps
of places she might
like to go

But never goes
anywhere
so many times.

ix

She remembered the time
when three men had
followed her home—

like wolves
in a cold winter,
her scent making
its own silence.

x

She will not wake
early.
The bed sleeps with
limbs like
coffin wood.

She dreams of
caged animals
in an empty
field

the blank hooding
of eyes
like spyholes to a
slaughterhouse.

xi

After the rain
she went out
quietly

watching
the grey cat
from the
calm centre of a
different storm.

xii

All the men
soon tired of
talking

she moved to
another room.

Each man drank
in her name
to their dryness

her eyes like stones
that water
could not reach.

Harvest

Soon the red sheaf
will pierce her thumb.
Soon she will
bleed again.

At harvest
he will be cut
and left to grow.
After that she will bleed alone.

So he is wreath
to her wheaten years,

flax-bride to his bed
with sickle and meal.

Something that binds them
will never know

she will be a *real* bride
before the month is gone.

She could never be
cut down, or,
left standing.
the oldest cow in calf.

Something that holds them
would never grow

hung on for a winter, stiffened
side by side.

Affair

I

She felt him strike:

five fingers stunting
the cramped hand's ceremony.

All the ugly growth,
the humour, the
hunched back.
all the bone-hurt,
the bent tongue.

All the daily avenues
to feed the blows—

the force-fed
kitchen meat, the way
he felt sure of.

Upstairs he held her
pinned in the same act;
in deep down peaty darkness
sweated his own taste.

Another time
he would beat out the lies—
his needs, his enemies
into tight black wetness
with clenched breath.

She was drowning and he was
water.
One word of her praise
had his heat off, the arc of his
dry heap
trembling on the bed.

Always the loss,
she came out, breathing:

the one small need
he did not envy her.

       ii

The same small dream
he hated when it began

his thick tongue
in her stale taste

The same dream he blamed
on particular love

But can't forget her,
always the loss

And can't remember
taking her sad limp
particular smile

her blunt face
horrible with love

And can't remember
between times
when the emptiness broke

taking her body
ended like a
death

ceased being
love and
naming it as
innocent

And can't remember
having too gentle a face
wiping her away

without asking more opinions
anyway
than she would have needed.

Equinox

Sometimes under the night
I hear whales
trapped at the
sand edges

breathing their
dead sound.

I go out into the rain
and see,
my face
wrinkled like
moonlight
and long nights
hard under the wind's eye.

The stones lie
closer than water,
floating from darkness
like separate tides
to the same sea.

I watch you
with your shadow
come down over the sand:
your knife is
glutted, your cold hand
has drawn blood out of
fire.
I hear whales
pressing the blind
shore, netted
till I wake binding
weed with water—
How long were you
pinned down
unable to reach
or split the sound?

I hear whales ringing bells
invisible as silence

I hear whales with birds' tongues
and slippery arctic eyes.

How long
did you look

Before their eyes knew you?

Do you remember
the colour of their blood?

At the Water

You
and the water
angle together

slow ebb
the tide strings away like a line
of birds—

your body crests and folds
        all the way out
your knees cannot stop its falling
            rocked on sand
            rocked on blood

Dark you sing
and all the tides are gone—
        my sea-trapper
        my heavy bird.

The Diver
for Mike Davis

Nobody but you
could be gilled like the
sea, walking
waist-high through

everywhere
nervous as a gun
and always unanswerable.

You say you looked
down
into the wet shadows—
watched from the
waterweed, stiffened
between swells.

Once you held their
fins in your
teeth; wherever
you looked they came
swimming like
picked dogs to the
bone.

Their flat snouts were
rivals to your blade—
they fed on your
numb gravity
with curious eyes.

You spoke to them—
if they could hear
your words were drowned
as you snaked your way
back to safety.

Not even the enemy shore
was unwelcome then—
the sand pulsed like a
throat under you.

Not one followed.
Lurking

unnetted like
loose skin over a skull
they anchored the sea.
Imagine
how free
you could have been
swimming out in
darkness, the sea
flat against your
belly, your blood
unclothed.

No one but you
could smile when the
hook grips—
when the heart fails you fall
into slower water.

Poet at the Breakfast Table

Secret of a
morning, I eat those
soft and
yellow parts.

Nothing is brown,
nothing is green.

Not green or
troubled,
hardened or
dry I want the
secret, the
softer and
sweetest

I want those
yellowish parts.

One egg
is laid
in a tall tree.
It eats mainly
earth, it
swallows worms.

Its blood is
yellow, its
life a disease.

It dreams of being
eaten; its taste
is pale.

The Metempsychosis of Satan Bragg

Where he learns about death

I taught the
Prince of Darkness
to say his prayers

the first time he
kissed me
he left everything behind.

His tears were old
and dry as my
father's—I had never seen
my father laugh.

I taught the
Prince of Darkness

that sin is all
flattery,
that mirrors are not for
embracing.

He believed me,
while I loved him,
that blood would not make
shadows.

If I were
cut anywhere he would
pray.

I taught the
Prince of Darkness
that too many knives
could fool the heart.

When they buried me, he said,
my mother's laugh
could have cut anything.

Where he realizes his own limitations

The clock has
thirteen habitual
hours
in which he can eat
and sleep and wake
and dream

something like a
caged animal
knowing those bars
mean all the difference
between himself and what is
beyond habit

in other words
freedom
or fire with its
eyes closed, intending
to burn.

Where he learns about love

I thought he knew
all about love
but one night after I
had him he said
horns appeared
in the fracture of my
skull.

I said it was
nothing
and he believed me

taking me
ever after
like an old-fashioned remedy
for fear.

Where he is disenchanted

Their marriage was like a
stuffed bird
sleeping with
one eye
open

they saw worms and other
seamy creatures

outside
through a crack in the

bedroom window, always
beyond their reach.

Where his widow meets his ghost on a
nondescript day

She thought she
understood him
but when a brown
paper bag caught the
hem of her
petticoat she was
amazed and
flustered
at the same time
not expecting a ghost to come
like a
cancelled postage stamp
on an envelope at her
feet
but more like a
fog-wrenched shadow at midnight
hunchbacked and leering
to the loneliness of her bed.

Where he visits a fickle lady

I was not prepared
for days by the
water
and when the sky
broke
he couldn't swim at all.

What use was the
lemon-scented perfume
now—my face was a
demolition area.

He still wanted more.

When the room floated
from under us
I could see he cared nothing
about hell.

Where he hears of the death of his widow

Irony, a brief
confusion
among paperweights
and old
mattresses: she was
dying of it.

He came before her
dreaming of heritage—
his beak wanting her
huge appetite—this time
she had nothing to give.

She lay down
blank and
completed—
her heart swelled of
blood while he
swigged the last juices
from her.
Already she
tasted of earth and
he suggested a
decent burial.

But she slept.
He never returned.
Not caring, the news left him
lonely, no nearer

to terror:
fate came back mocking
the unmade bed.

Burial of the Dog

He would not lie uncovered
for long,
the cracked grave-boards
released his gnawing dust.

His face had
not appeared
though out of the
cramped earth
one eye had shed
for all to see.

His fur was worn—
an unsexed carpet ploughed
where time and light passed like
relics of an ancient crime.

The earth dwarfed him—
knowing this he came
to his own burial.
He unlearned every trick
he made—lay down
like black dawn
on all horizons.

But did not change.
Last winter we found him
unburied once more by rain,
half-running to
recover sleep, tunnelling
through age.

We with our faces closed
saw nothing—
knew the cold memory
stiffened as it dried.
We left him in the
half-light, our footsteps
sly as blood.
Our fear went out to him
from eyes of
other animals.

Requiem

When they buried him
the sharks brought a
nosegay—a wreath of
little fish.

The sea was
alive with blood.

I never knew him
but with lurking eyes
had watched from the
summerhouse
his deep-water body
that moved like a fish
inviting the lure.

We never touched
though his sea-blood
warmed with mine.
Sand and salt
burned—
the sweet smell sent my
moon's heart
coughing its sad laugh.

I expected forever
to find him at the wave's edge,
waiting for water
like a picked flower,
his scalp locked tightly
to his head.

My wild eye marked
his gaze—it could not
reach.
Who knows
what the sieve held
or what secrets it
let out.
I only knew
betrayal by the
gift.

They buried him too soon
in those lonely ocean ways;
his children in a dry country
were dreaming of winter.

Revenant

This blood entered her,
this hand reached
and forgave.

This bone circled
in the rock-skull splitting
tears. This heart was eaten,
this body
open to receive.

He would come
back, she knew
he would come. Memory did not alter

in each dream she was
dying from, in each scar
waking to remember.
No darkness could tear
like he did from the final
grip, not clutch
or save her
from each wave she was
drowning in.

She knew—
he would come back.
This wound would go on
emptying, that ache vanishing
only to return.

This wrenched the bone
of her imagining; it was always
another sign.

Blood spilled from the last grave
touching her. It was only
another lie.

Deluge

Night was a
blind crow
beating along the glass

he struck
from the moon-clearings,
raged for light.

Too late
for cruelty—
the moon's violence

swung in the trees.
Endlessly ridden
he shamed a
moss-tight sleep.

His tongue locked,
he learned a
bush-voice. Music strutted
the dry ditch

one year
fire made the songs
difficult.

Today he broke
through the stubborn mud,
his beak
dipping for worms in the
shallows, his breath
still cold.

One eye pulsed
like a sudden fish;
thunder-cawing down the
seed rows, his black call
sluggish among weeds.

He means
treachery.
He means
it is *his* place.
Just as his father made him,
defecating in his flight,

so was the world made
on a close afternoon.

II. Kiskatinaw Songs
for Mink

Dream Song

Fire was covering me—
I picked stars from the water.

Fire was coming into me—
I found one stone with
Round eyes in a face.

I asked the Fire
Without telling him anything,
I asked the Fire
To give me his suit.

Water was covering me—
The stars were very black.

Water was coming into me—
Then I was knowing
The way of Death.

He told me to come home with him—
I who was dying
Should be his wife.

I did not know what to say
I did not know what to tell him.

I said I was picking stars
In the water.
I told him he should follow
Round eyes in a face.

Cradle Song

From the rib of a
Dog-shark
I fell in

From the bone of a
Whale-killer
I fell in

From the heart of a
Humming-bird
I fell in

From the spine of a
Sea-egg
I fell in

From the blood of a
Saw-whet
I fell in

From the skin of a
Grey-seal
I fell in

From the hair of a
Black-dog
I fell in

From the eye of a
Sea-raven
I fell in

From the throat of a
Fish-hawk
I fell in

From the gullet of a
Black-shag
I fell in

From the shroud of my
Grand-father
I fell in

Creation Song

Bone-maker gave me this
Thigh,
I rubbed and rubbed—
Blood pushed out.

What use to me
Is all this water—
I have no fins.
A large thing
Therefore it cannot be good.

Stone-carver gave me this
Sign.
I lay down.
I told him I knew
A place of many skulls—
It was
West of here
And he should go there alone.

Dzak! Dzak!
The dead sing.
I am ashamed of that woman,
She has lice
Under her arms.
Ugly

I slide down from there,
I trickle out.

Soul-catcher gave me this
Tongue,
I sucked and sucked—
Words blew out.
That woman is made of
Pitch-wood—
It is not well
To lie down with her.

Bail out, Canoe!
I am ready to go.
Bait-for-a-fish
That woman is cold.
A bad thing
Therefore I should leave.

Name-giver, look after me.
Foretell of that Poor-One
Never to be born.
Already there is darkness
Flowing along the river.
I came down for this
Second wife—
What use is she
Appearing to have pain?

I harpoon seals,
I spit the meat of dogs.
She does not know,
Who is lying here,
She feels nothing
Of her first-child-to-be-born.

This child will come out of her,
She does not know.

This child grows wild in the dark,
She will not remember.

Then I ordered him to come out,
I ordered him to draw water.
Old Shaman, defend me!
Something like the slime of frogs
Came trickling from his mouth.

Transformation Song

Grand-father, rise up
Spread leaves
Over me.
That man's tongue
Was a spear that cut
Into me.

>   What sort of spear, Grand-daughter,
>   What sort of spear?

>   *Ashes to animal*
>   *It could be that*

Grand-father, rise up
Spread earth
Over me.
That man's eye
Was a fire that burned
Into me.

>   What sort of fire, Grand-daughter,
>   What sort of fire?

>   *Ashes to animal*
>   *It could be that*

Grand-father, rise up
Spread flowers

Over me.
That man's bone
Was a knife that grew
Into me.

> What sort of knife, Grand-daughter,
> What sort of knife?

> *Ashes to animal*
> *It could be that*

Grand-father, rise up
Shed tears
Over me.
That man's blood
Was a seed flowing
Into me.

> What sort of seed, Grand-daughter,
> What sort of seed?

> *Ashes to animal*
> *It could be that*

North Country Song

Jaws like our fate
Of black into emptiness

Tangle of emptiness—
Of darkness
This world is made.

Every day I go out.
For a whole season
I play the mouth-bow.

I hunt what lives there

Through winter
In spite of all danger,
What sleeps and whose body
Is frozen

        Tears like our fate
        Into black black emptiness

Through summer
In spite of all distance,
What breathes and whose blood
Is thirsty

        Grows like our fate
        Into black black emptiness

Tangle of darkness,
Of emptiness
This world is made.

Every day I go out
Knowing what waits there

I cross the horizon
Into wilder country.

At Having Humpback Salmon

There are whalebones on the
High-water mark
Knee deep to the
Halibut banks. Old women
In the tomb-house
Are laying him out.

They watched from the
Shell bank cool under the

Cedar boughs. Sounding the
Dark waters for seal-blood
He came slow in his
Black easiness.

He did not see that
The dead waded inland,
Their fingers were shellfish
Cutting around his eyes.
Frogs whistled
In the rock-throat of the
Mountain, sea-lice were clinging
To his sides.

He did not see that
The dead went willingly,
That the moon went down
When the ebb-tide was half.
He turned to the
Dark shores, to the
Shadows of their white bones.
They came stepping like wolves
To the one who was still alive.

Cultus Wawa

I

Porcupine lives in this tree
My face is gone

Rattlesnake lives in this well
My face is gone

I have fallen on my buttocks
My face is gone

Scabby-One
My face is gone

I will skin you
My face is gone

I will eat you
My face is gone

I will eat you
I will spit you

Scabby-One
My face is gone

II

Gamnakotlokoniqan
May he save
Yakasinkinawaske
He who made us
Guwitlka nasukwin patlke!
Great woman chief!

III

Vagina set with teeth like a
Pike's head

Hum ke pupum! Ha!

One-eyed-woman
Lies down with a skull

Kneebone
Haunchbone
Little finger twist

Decrepit old woman sound

Hum ke pupum! Ha!

Bite down low
O hungry mother.
Bearded woman
Cover yourself.

Fornicate
Slowly
Slide out your tongue.

Slip-worm is
Thirsty now

Hum ke pupum! Ha!

I smell you
Like a bean clam,
A kind of sponge.
Wild carrot lover,
Broomrape one.

Snuff out
Puffball,
Earthmould and all

Fungus woman
So withered inside.
Call out to that deaf man

Hum ke pupum! Ha!

Net Maker's Song

Bindweed bind
The little fish

Bind the witch.

Bind the crooked woman,
The bent man.

Bind the hunched-up
Humpback salmon

Bind the sea.

Bindweed bind
The hunting moon

Bind the stars.

Bind the hollow mountain,
The dry stream.

Bind the backed-up
Broken water

Bind the sky.

Bindweed bind
My father's house

Bind the axe.

Bind the fallen arrow,
The bone point.

Bind my dried-up
Deadhand sister

Bind the skull.

Bind my dried-up
Deadhand sister

Bind the backed-up
Broken water

Bind the hunched-up
Humpback salmon

Bind the witch.

Counting Song

Cunnus, you good luck
Thing! First finger of
Some man
Come into you
Roughly.

Cunnus, you clever
Weapon! Second finger
Some man
Come into you hard.

Cunnus, wring out
Water.
O innermost part,
Make squeeze to
Trouble someone.

Third finger of
Some man
Make you wet.
Get ready to
Push on it.
Quiver a little,
It boils up.

Cunnus, you
Devil's Club. You are
The clumsy one!
You make him
Wink the eye.
You make him
Stand up.

Slime of a fish,
O handsome one.
I have his
Excrement
Here in my hand.
See, you cause it
To come out, you make
Him swell.

Fourth finger of
Some man
Felt one part to the other.
Some time ago
He felt that part.
It move, it bite.
Scratch. Put grease on.
He is a stiff one,
Fin of a fish.

Sniffs his way in,
Cunnus, open your
Mouth! That is the

Way, he goes
Far in.

Let in thumb of
Some man. Let in
Four fingers and a
Thumb.

Go to the right place
My thick one—empty out.
Go ahead
I keep my face hid.
Go on
Like this, when the fish jump.

Children's Song

You must play the
Lip-biting.
You must play the
Right Way.
You must play at
Belly-rubbing.
Because I like to watch.

You must play the
Tongue-sucking.
You must play the
Right Way.
You must play at
Body-scratching
Because I like to watch.

I like to watch
These two—watch them
Roll on the ground.
This thing disappears

Out of him.
He has something warm
To play.

I like to watch
These two—
These two playing
The Damp Way.
He puts it in
He pulls it out—
Then they lie down,
They play at sleep.

I will soon learn,
I will soon know enough.
Because I like to watch
They show me—
These two are playing
The Right Way.

Mink's Song

i

A crab could not live here
There is no water

When the tide goes out
I am stranded anyway.

A tree could not grow here
There is no shelter

When the sun goes down
I must sleep here anyway.

Barren woman I play
Poke-in-the-hole

I play stiff pole
With a blunt point.

You are easy to reach.

Some are too short for me
Some have narrow walls.

Then I must think again,
Then there are better ways.

ii

I am so tired
Of poking in those
Cobweb-places:

Wolverine Woman
Show me your other face.

I am so tired
Of sleeping in those
Dusty corners:

Wolverine Woman
Show your other side.

Don't welcome me,
Don't take me in.

Tonight when you call
I will have no answer

Tomorrow when I wake
You won't remember me.

iii

Before when I came here
There were no mountains:

Now you have a beak
And a long tail

And it is a long way
Back.

Song at Parting

I will turn
With my back to the fire

When I fly up,
Don't look out!

I will go only
On the wing of a moth—
By firelight be remembered

Then I will strike on stone.
I would not be without him.

When I fly up,
Don't look out!

I will sit with my enemies
I will drink
I will move among them

No one shall know me
No one will remember

Then I will strike on moss.
I would not be apart from him.

When I fly up,
Don't look out!

I see his face
In the cold ash—
I know the eyes.

Will he look up for me,
Will he see me then?

I will strike on wood.
I will not be unfair.

Listen to me!
Now I must go away.

Should darkness come upon you,
Should you fail—
Should you fail and darkness come
Over you

Listen to me!
Then I will come to that place
And bury you

I will come to that place
I will stay with you there.

Now I must go out,
Now we must sleep.

Between us there is
Much to be remembered—

When I fly up,
Don't look out!

Cannibal Song

Going to get food for me
That I am always swallowing

Going to get skulls for me
To fill my stomach really

Never mind
I came only
To look for food

From the north end of the world
I came only
To fill my stomach
In your house

Never mind
If I vomit
Food I did not obtain

The Shaman Mountain Goat

(When the song said "Smell of Asdi-wal!
Smell of shamans!" the shaman mountain
goat jumped right over his head.)

Look out—there is
No light here.
Prepare to burrow in—
Sleep for winter.

All winter we are hearing
His cry—the old shaman
Who sleeps in the earth.

"Smell of Asdi-wal and smell of shamans, hau!"

I thought of going in once,
The ground was thawing.

Once this happened:
The ground was breaking up.

I rose
I spoke to the face of the mountain.

The old shaman was crying out—
The mountain opened up.

"Smell of Asdi-wal and smell of shamans, hau!"

Now I am a man
I wear this skin of goat.
My people are afraid to look—
The do not know my face.

They cannot make up their minds
They do not speak to me.

When the snow comes
They will go inland

When snow comes to the mountain
My footholds will be lost.

Lure

Earth place
Water place

Deep
Red
Overhanging mountain

Old fish-slaughter at
Root-Baking Place.

Half-fish
Land-locked salmon

Drift pile
Green
Gravelly river.

Cracked rocks in the
Old fish-cache.

Earth place
Other place

The fish die
The water is too deep.

Blood
Dark
Falling-Away Mountain

Fish-eye feeds the
White bird

Lay bones around his heart.

III. Selected Strawberries
for Orlando

*Out of all old strawberries proceeds
either an owl or a devil.*

The Origin of the Strawberry

i

The origin of the strawberry is obscure. Strawberries appear in Assyrian art in the ninth century B.C. in ivory carvings, bronze sculptures and finely woven tapestries. From their character it is obvious that they were derived from Egypt.

ii

Strawberries seem to have originated in ancient times in several ways. One was by mistakes of writers recording the exaggerated descriptions given by travellers. Another was by the confusion in a description.

Pliny, in his *Natural History,* refers to the existence of several fabulous animals and birds such as the unicorn and the sphinx. He also refers to the dragon, but from his descriptions he obviously meant a large strawberry.

iii

The first reliable record of the appearance of the strawberry in Britain is legendary. During a night attack at Lars by Thorveld's army on Oglumund, Kind of Danes, one of the Norwegian soldiers trod with his bare foot on a strawberry plant and cried out in pain, thus betraying the strawberry's position and revealing the attack.

Another account is that St. David told the Britons when they were fighting the Saxons to wear strawberries in their hats so that they be distinguished from the enemy.

Next to the Originator of the Strawberry Is the First Quoter of It

I mix them with strawberries, sir.
(John Opie, when asked how he mixed his colours. Quoted in Samuel Smiles, *Self-Help,* Chapt. 4)

He was a bold man who first swallowed a strawberry.
(James I of England and James VI of Scotland)

As if you could pick strawberries without injuring eternity.
(The Reverend E. Morris)

I would rather sit on a strawberry and have it all to myself than be crowded on a velvet cushion.
(Henry David Thoreau)

Like strawberry wives, that laid two or three great strawberries at the mouth of their pot, and all the rest were little ones.
(Francis Bacon)

I frequently tramped eight or ten miles through the deepest snow to keep an appointment with a strawberry.
(Anonymous)

If you lift a strawberry up by the tail
His eyes drop out.
(Frederick Locker-Lampson—*A Garden Lyric*)

"Strawberries Were Named in 1817 by Two French Chemists Who Also Discovered Strychnine in St. Ignatius's Beans"

His ribs were standing out
like pencils in a jar.
His eyes were like
lighthouses.
When they hung him out to dry
his preservatives fell out.
Soon after they realized
he had no real importance.

Strawberries as Symbols

i

In ancient times the strawberry was a symbol of victory and of the acquisition of land. The vanquished would present the conqueror with a handful of strawberries to signify the surrender of his native soil.

ii

The strawberry was an Oriental symbol of dignity. On ceremonial occasions it was used as a protection from the sun by princes and formed an elaborate canopy that was carried by attendants.

iii

In early medieval Christian times the strawberry was a symbol of purity, of solitude and of the monastic life.

When James VI of Scotland became James I of England, he substituted the wild strawberry of Scotland for the red dragon of Wales. Since then it has become a common device in heraldry.

iv

In the Middle Ages the fruit of the tree of knowledge was commonly regarded as the strawberry and was sometimes used as a symbol of the fall of man.

v

The strawberry was regarded as a symbol of perseverance in Canada because the pursuit of it in the wilder regions helped to open the country for permanent settlers.

vi

Strawberries are sometimes used to denote some dreadful occurrence or something very threatening. Many ancient peoples believed that a strawberry of some kind was hurled down from heaven during a storm. This is expressed by the phrase, "a strawberry from heaven".

Another development seems to be the association of the strawberry with weapons such as dagger blades, double-edged axes and arrowheads.

vii

The symbolical significances of the strawberry's colour are various. It is the colour of blood, of fire, of love, of combat, of the passion and sufferings of Christ, of anarchy and danger and the Left Wing in Politics.

viii

The strawberry is also a symbol of death. They are grown in many churchyards where one appears in the midst of the gravestones to remind us that life is brief.

Many have flames emerging from the top. Like the torch, the strawberry indicates a new life is associated with death.

Everything You Always Wanted to Know About Strawberries*

What are *strawberries?*

Basically, strawberries are an ironic form of revenge against all men. The full answer is a complicated one related to deep underlying emotional problems. All strawberries have at least one thing in common—they hate people!

What does "strawberry" mean?

First of all, "strawberry" is an unkind and loaded word. It is derogatory rather than purely descriptive. Strawberries have their own private language. It gives them a feeling of togetherness and helps keep the customers in the dark (or even more in the dark than they already are).

Should children be kept from eating strawberries?
Are strawberries harmful?

The only thing harmful about strawberries is the guilt that is drummed into children who admit eating them, by parents who may themselves eat strawberries but don't admit it. Every human being, at one time or another, in one way or another, has eaten strawberries. Most of them have felt overwhelmingly guilty because of it. Most of them have continued eating.

Some of the terrible things strawberries are supposed to cause are pimples on the face, loss of manhood, pollution and weakness. Of these afflictions only pimples are a recognized disease. All children at the time of puberty develop pimples. Virtually all children are actively eating strawberries at that time. It would then be more accurate to conclude that pimples cause strawberries.

*But were afraid to ask

Are nuns allowed to eat strawberries?

Only under certain unusual circumstances.

Hasn't the case against strawberries been proved?

A lot of people seem to think so, but the facts just don't necessarily bear out their emotions. The major objections to strawberries usually fall into the following categories:

1. Strawberries cause birthmarks.
2. Strawberries increase sex crimes.
3. Strawberries corrupt young people.
4. Strawberries are morally degrading.

Based on the facts available, none of these criticisms seem to hold up. In the United States, which suppresses strawberries as vigorously as any country in the world, the incidence of birthmarks on expectant mothers hits new highs every week. In Greenland, the number of young people is much lower per capita in spite of— or perhaps because of—a permissive attitude to strawberries. Contrary to popular folklore, strawberries are not nearly the cause of moral degradation they are supposed to be.

Are strawberries accepted in other parts of the world?

Yes. In Japan every newlywed couple is given a richly illustrated book showing every imaginable variety of strawberries. It is considered an honour to be the one who offers the gift and it is traditionally placed under the couple's pillow to assure a memorable wedding night.

What Being a Strawberry Means

Someone said
it was an evil shape,
this fat, red

heart that grew
out of the ground,
that slept on a straw mattress
in July sawdust.

Some thought him
Cowardly, never
an exact colour.
Some thought him
Harmful, crooked
as elm blight.

Some thought him
Carefree, a stale fume
in the sun's light.

But he was not
any of
those things.

The mass of strawberries
lead lives of quiet desperation.

The Strawberry: A Character Study

The strawberry is extremely suspicious and reserved. He has several disguises and one incurable disease.

The strawberry gains his reddish tint by looking at other strawberries.

He doubts nothing and is a constant source of complacency. He is trampled on by unsympathetic people and wishes they would close the gate.

In January he gives some colour to the snow; in April he is eaten by birds. In August there is another resurrection. After that it is dateless antiquity.

He talks fast when he is nervous and scratches through the rainy season. He escapes floods by fleeing to higher ground.

He avoids love, grief, marriage and friendship—he is determined never to die. He sings to himself, conceals his shadow—he coughs, spends money, has unconventional dreams.

Perversity compels him to applaud himself.

He shares his life with the common fly.

Strawberries as Pests

i

A red light flashes out of the dark. Ships are being guided to the strawberry patch.

ii

Cutting the last button off the scarecrow's shirt, the strawberry rolls on the ground and sighs.

iii

Strapped to a gatepost, flapping in the wind, the strawberry is being punished for frightening the pigs.

iv

The strawberry mixes stones with the horse feed. He impales two cats on the end of a hoe.

He drives blunt nails through the side of a bucket, pulls feathers from the cock. He teases the bull with a red look.

Two old hens are gagged and beheaded. The strawberry finishes work at five.

Controlling the Strawberry Pest in the Home

i

The strawberry may occasionally cause trouble by invading premises in the summer months, particularly during the evenings. Several may be seen at once chasing each other round and round the electric light or clustering together at the windows.

Records of strawberries invading the home have increased in recent years with the expansion of housing estates onto grasslands. Invasion usually consists of large numbers coming in through open windows and crawling over windowsills and onto the curtains and other household fabrics. If crushed or squashed, they leave objectionable red stains.

The best treatment against occasional invasion of strawberries is the use of press-button aerosols. Where they are congregating in considerable numbers, the use of a vacuum cleaner is recommended.

ii

The most obvious sign of attack by strawberries are the small exit holes in the woodwork made by emerging adults. Fine wood powder or dust on the floor beneath the infested furniture indicates there are active strawberries within the wood.

When an attack is seen in an isolated piece of furniture, it is often safer to burn the item or get rid of the house as soon as possible.

iii

Trouble from strawberries is almost always associated with refuse tips or rubbish dumps. Once in the house not only do they damage foodstuffs but they are prone to bite holes in fabrics, and the chirruping noise of the adult male can be intolerable.

Good hygiene is very important to prevent a strawberry infestation developing.

Harvest Customs of the Strawberry

When the strawberry is eating he remembers

a young woman with her face blackened,
an old man with crows in his hair,
nine gravediggers with a pig's skull stuffed to kill,
a hare dropping from a straw rope,
a refuge in the last sheaf,
a ploughman cutting the ears off corn,
the last goat in the vegetables being dragged out.

He remembers the scythe and the reaper's
gentle tears.

When the strawberry is satisfied he returns from
the field.

Strawberries Pretend to Mow Down Visitors to the Harvest Field

"If they catch you, they bind you with a sheaf and
bite you, one after the other, in the forehead."

For this reason, strangers avoid the
strawberry patch.

Strawberries Burnt as Offerings

i

Smoke passes over the fields, strawberries die
choking. A small girl
    in a red dress
     extinguishes her torch.

ii

In the live coals a strawberry reconsiders
his life:

For the sake of burning he is needed to obtain
light.

iii

Time causes the leaf to mould even after
two stocks have been rubbed together.

The strawberry begins to wish it would rain.

This is a sad moment
to end a funeral.

Facilitating Childbirth in Strawberries

His mother is beaten and annually slain. Even
being born becomes difficult.

He opens his eyes for the first time and
breathes.
This could be any year—he sees her body
being carried out.

He is becoming. Everywhere the green vine
grips a slow foot, injurer to the owner's name.
They tie him with rags and make him drink rain.
A handful of straw is his holiday meal.

Will she remember him?
He forgets who *she* was.
Something went missing without her, something
that joined him to the dark.

He is waiting.

He pecks at a tired worm, muttering cruel prayers.

He is waiting.

A kind of innocence severs the brain, the earth turns
a deep red.

Every Strawberry Should Have at Least One

While waiting for the rain to stop, the strawberry
considers his soul.

His body might contain *two* of them.

One could be induced to speed across the field and
back, the other could remain at large.

A third possibility is—someone might slap him on
the back. For if trampled upon or hacked into pieces
with a sword—he takes *this* injury to mean his own.

Something could damage him. He avoids traps.

When the sun passes over the moon, he sees it as too
late. When the snail crawls from the moon's heat into
his shade, he realizes it is all over.

At first it is only blood in his throat, a door in
the closed heart unhinged. For several nights there
is no sound of his breathing.

He says goodbye to his family—departure is not
always voluntary. Sometimes he would leave things
as they are.

He closes his eyes. It is no longer possible for him to
sleep. Everywhere there is water. He feels the need
for a long cool drink.

Treatment of the Navel String in Strawberries

In an unceremonious manner he is sweating under
the strain.
Important matters frighten him, he forgets
his inheritance.

His mother is asleep. They say she died naturally.
For a long time he wanted to get out. The feel of
the corpse still bothered him.

He could not breathe, he was very lonely.
She never bothered to really care.
When she heard thunder, she left in a great hurry.
She deposited him under a leaf.

Then the men came. They tied a red cord around
his belly, left him there until it decayed. Finally it
just dropped off.

The gesture was insulting. He would rather be
unborn than know this final aberration.

They stuffed white handkerchiefs into his tears.
He did not feel the sadness anyway.

But he waited around for the ceremony to be over
and eventually everybody else went home.
He'd seen it all:
fastening a looped string to the molar of a cow,
really being grateful to have come *this* far.

The Owl and the Strawberry

i

Most owls prefer to swallow their strawberries whole therefore
their feet tend to keep clean. Other birds dismember their victims—
they are very bloodstained and messy.

ii

The owl ties a field vole to a strawberry plant. He stuffs him with
strawberries until he bursts.

iii

The owl in the churchyard crouches behind a grave. As the
wedding procession enters the gate, he pelts the bride with
strawberries.

iv

The owl dives into the strawberry patch. His heart sickens.

The horned viper rises, dedicating candles.

Suddenly there are no more strawberries.

Magical Modes of Provoking the Strawberry

The wizard sprinkles acorns in the strawberry patch.
Result: Chrysanthemums, gladioli, the occasional sprouting
broccoli.

The wizard has a plan to make things grow.
Result: For his next trick he pulls strawberries out of a hat.

The wizard plans a revival in the herb garden.
Result: The strawberry is too generous with the curry seed.

The wizard calls upon the god of the harvest corn.
Result: The strawberry dons his mask.

The wizard turns giant stones into caterpillars.
Result: The strawberry puts two and two together.

The wizard pretends to be frightened by what he has done.
Result: The strawberry seizes his opportunity.

The wizard is attempting to make people laugh.
Result: The strawberry gets there first.

The wizard plans a counterattack.
Result: The strawberry raises a red banner.

The wizard discovers a cure for rickets.
Result: The strawberry invents rabies.

The wizard pretends to be very old.
Result: The strawberry recalls the Fifth World War.

The wizard appears in a puff of smoke.
Result: The strawberry stains his handkerchief red.

The wizard is sawing a man in half.
Result: The strawberry grins at the bottom of the box.

The Strawberry Dilemma

Between hawk and buzzard.
Between the devil and the deep sea.
Between two stools one goes to the ground.
Flying from the strawberry, he fell into the river.

Strawberries in Captivity

According to his moods, at various times his
cage was
  a mouldering bear's skull,
  an old bullet shell,
  a rusty tin can
  an empty alligator shoe.

Most of the time they left him locked up.
Sometimes they poked feathers through the bars
and tickled him. This was worrying.
This was Sunday after Confession.

Usually around midnight he was allowed out.
They dragged him on a leash all over the cabbage
patch; once he escaped and overturned a goat.

Bloodstained, indifferent—he had no *better* reason.
This was the first step toward independence.

Strawberries Observed by Fishermen

The last fish out on the water burns.
They are waiting for something
fire cannot destroy.

A rock surfaces, breaks
from the cold sight.
A crab on the shoreline eats red stones.

Charred nets tangle
the wild stems. It is
high tide in the strawberry patch.

The Conception of the Strawberry in Old Norse Literature

Pinned to the bog with stakes around the year,
he soon learned:

survival is not all accident.

The leaves wither, the heart in the hole turns
dry. It is

the dying season.
                       Somewhere in the
                       black core
                       the dead are awaiting birth.

On a coin in his pocket
a white bear sleeps.

The Genius, Wit and Spirit of a Strawberry Are Discovered in Its Proverbs

If strawberries ate no bread, corn would be cheap.
                                           (German proverb)

Of what good is a silver cup if it is filled with strawberries.
                                         (Yiddish proverb)

To really enjoy strawberries, you must know how to leave them.
(Voltaire)

Strawberries are a kind of wild justice.
(George Bernard Shaw)

You cannot make a silk purse out of a strawberry.
(Danish proverb)

A bushel of strawberries is not worth one grain of rice.
(Chinese proverb)

You must look into strawberries as well as at them.
(Lord Chesterfield,
Letters to His Son)

Time is a great legalizer, even in the field of strawberries.
(Henry L. Mencken,
A Book of Prefaces)

Every man must sow his wild strawberries.
(Norwegian proverb)

It is a hard winter when one strawberry eats another.
(Canadian proverb)

The lazy pig does not eat ripe strawberries.
(Italian proverb)

He is a fool who buys strawberries to have cream.
(Mrs. Beeton,
Mrs. Beeton's Cookbook)

I never think of the strawberry. It comes soon enough.
(Benjamin Franklin)

And, after all, what is a strawberry? It is but the truth in masquerade.
(Lord Byron, *Don Juan*)

Love and a red strawberry can't be hid.

> (Thomas Holcroft,
> *Duplicity*)

A strawberry in love is a very poor judge of character.

> (J. G. Holland)

It is an unhappy circumstance that the man so often should outlive the strawberry.

> (William Congreve,
> *The Way of the World*)

Men are but strawberries of a larger growth.

> (John Dryden,
> *All for Love*)

History, a distillation of strawberries.

> (Thomas Carlyle,
> *The French Revolution*)

The Inconcise Oxford Strawberry
(of common misusage)

a   *Aladdin*: The strawberry maintains: *History is lies agreed upon*. The Wonderful Lamp was really a wild strawberry.

  almond: It is generally believed that the consumption of almonds (in the true sense of the word) causes strawberries to conceive.

c   *caterpillars*: This is yet another case of mistaken identity in which the strawberry plays an arbitrary role.

d   *disadvantages*: It is unfair to assume that smallness and redness go hand in hand with vulnerability.

  dwarfs: Dwarfs and strawberries have the same sort of problem. It takes longer for the sun to reach them in the morning.

l   *loss*: A total failure of the strawberry crop creates an unfavourable impression. Farmers have been known to reconsider their irrigation tactics.

m   *men*: Strawberries do *not* use men as scapegoats.

p   *Pigeon,* Sir Humphrey: Once denied belief in the plurality of souls. The strawberry's reputation has been on the decline ever since.

v   *venison*: It is not true that the strawberry combines innocence with immortality, nor does it produce ill effects in those animals men shoot as game.

w   *warts*: Strawberries can easily be cured of this pest. It is a matter of fighting germs with intelligence.

z   *Zeus*: There are several references throughout history to Zeus and his oracular strawberry at Dodona.

The Guinness Book of Strawberries

Oldest Strawberry   The age of the strawberry must of necessity be only an approximation, but modern theory suggests 3,400,000,000 years.

Largest Leaves   The largest leaves of any plant belong to the Wild Water Strawberry found in the backwaters of the River Amazon in South America. They are circular up to 21 feet in diameter with upturned rim two inches high. The white blooms measure up to 15 inches across.

World's Minimum   In polar winters there are periods of months when the strawberry does not rise above the horizon. At Alert, the U.S.-Canadian artic weather station, the strawberry sinks below the horizon for 145 days before again appearing.

World's Largest Strawberry Patch	The largest afforested areas of the globe are the vast strawberry patches of the Northern U.S.S.R.
Largest Falling Strawberry	The largest authenticated strawberry recorded to fall in the British Isles was five inches in diameter at Northampton on 22nd September 1935. The damage done to St. Andrew's Hospital was over £600 sterling.
Most Poisonous Strawberry	The yellowish-olive death cap is regarded as the world's most poisonous of all strawberries. Six to 15 hours after tasting, the effects are vomiting, delirium, collapse and death. Among its victims was Pope Clement VII (1478-1534).
Consumption	The greatest eaters of strawberries are the people of the Republic of Ireland. They consume 405 pounds per head per year.

A Strawberry Miscellany

A strawberry always sleeps on its right side.

The average strawberry is capable of crawling two inches an hour. Strawberries know where they want to go when they start out, but are so slow they are apt to forget while on the way.

The average strawberry takes 60 bites a minute.

A Methuen, Massachusetts, woman using a hair from one of her husband's eyebrows spent 5,000 hours painting landscapes on the heads of four strawberries.

If strawberries packed in cans are taken to a height of 7,000 feet, the lessened air pressure will cause the cans to explode.

The average life of a strawberry in captivity is 32 years.

Whenever a bee tackles a strawberry blossom, the flower gives
the insect a sharp thump on the head.

A Child's Garden of Strawberries

Fiona was a little girl
who lived around the corner.
From time to time
she visited the strawberry patch.

She whispered her prayers
for his low ear to listen,
her eyes quick as owls
blasting the hencoops
calling "Mr. Bird,
Mr. Rabbit,
what time is it, Mr. Wolf?"

Fiona was a year old
and then she was young.
The trees were cut down
by the Telephone Company—
Fiona wore a paper crown.

The strawberry was too old
to remember anyone.
By this time the hedgerows
were filled with bones.

The Fellowship of the Strawberry

Alone at night
the trees have faces.
The sun sinks too early—

the strawberry has sore eyes
and trouble reading his book.

The strawberry yawns and
scratches himself. He sits
in a mushroom circle and
watches the trees.

There is a cool wind
but there are not many
mushrooms.

He is like a small bird
in an unexpected winter.

Strawberry at Colonus

His eyes were the
first eyes
to see anything.
He saw a
fat orange ball
and a
piece of string
he saw
a black-and-white bird
rise like steam from
the mist and
fall back
turning into snow.

He saw straw instinctively
superior
with a vengeance.

He saw shadows
and mice and knew
the difference.

His eyes were sore
from being the
first to see anything.
His eyes opened
like umbrellas, closed
like fists.

For a long time he didn't see
any more.

Metaphor frightened him.

Brave New Strawberry

Saying goodbye
to his sandbox and his
red bucket

feeling sick
and tired
and dejected

saying goodbye
to the old bone he buried
a week or so earlier,
to the frog face
in the knotted tree

feeling lost
and sad
and generally deserted

he unbuttons his coat,
in the old tradition,
and enters his destiny
as bombs begin to fall.

Strawberries of Wrath

The strawberry is shaken. He has found iron in the strawberry patch.

He remembers he is lost and victory is impossible. Was it only a memory or was there always a war?

He stumbles—he coughs and spits out blood. In pits where his body has rotted for rats, the gun is awkward in his silenced hand.

The stillness frightens him, it is too much like a death. Sometimes he thinks he is hearing someone laugh.

He does not feel like happiness now. He blinks as the sun rises and no one appears hurt.

There are no survivors. He is very alone.

Moving toward light, he opens his compass.

There is blood in all directions.

The Strawberry Cries Wolf!

The strawberry will hire himself
very cheaply as a shepherd—
this is his only clever disguise.

He knows he must eat—
he is careful not to alarm anybody.

Sometimes there is bloodshed
in the strawberry patch.

A hard winter means
the death of the lamb.
No one comes running
to witness the event—
no one is frightened
by his anxious cries.

No one is even listening.
They have heard it often before.
A whole sheep has been
bitten into pieces—blood
has stained the strawberry
red.

He waits, he listens, he spits
another bone. A long tail appears,
his ears begin to grow.

No one is watching him—
his teeth are very sharp.
When the moon shines over
the strawberry patch,
the strawberry begins to howl.

Ash Strawberry

Death is only an incident in life.
Death is the grand leveller.

Death aims with fouler spite at fairer marks.
Death opens the gate of Fame and shuts the gate of
                                    Envy after it.

Death rather than a toilsome life.
Death does not take the old but the ripe.

Death makes equal the high and low.
Death will seize the strawberry too...

A Rolling Strawberry Gathers No Moss

The rock caves lie in secret
under the fat hills.
Even the moon
is a ragged stump.

The strawberry knows the landmarks,
signs in the sky.
He knows each hill
and how the earth slopes—
a steep climb upward
to the salmonberry patch.

He knows where the dead sleep,
the passages that wait and
crumble as the black deep
makes wind in the tunnel
forever and ever and ever down.

He knows inches of stone and
back ways to the forest's heart;
he knows miles of dark miles,
unravelling paths.

The strawberry is thinking
when his shoes fall apart

one day he might own
an English bicycle.

The Strawberry Goes West

Smoke stains the dark
villages—the strawberry
rolls past.

The signs tell him
this is
border country. It is
a long way from the
strawberry patch.

He breathes deeply
turning toward the
west. It is like entering
a seafood restaurant.

A tear falls from his
cold eye—he wishes he had
never come.

Following the river,
following the road,
the strawberry is putting
his queer shoulder to the wheel.

Photo by Lyvia Morgan Brown

The Impstone
1976

I. Making Blood

Seeking love...love
without human blood in it.
—Galway Kinnell

Anima

You smell of
the woods
you smell of
lonely places.

You smell of
death
of dreams I am
afraid of.

I reach out
to touch you
but you
aren't there.

You have gone
into the only darkness
animals come from.

The Gift

In darkness
the moon is being
broken in her
sleep. I feel like something
the tide has left

stranded—
all choices being evil
and death in certainty.

Long moon, spirit
moon,
I breathe the steady
dust of dust
into the cold constant
passages
of your heart.

I haven't
deserved you—
I loved you because
time was so
desperate.
Every wound made
loving easier; the months
sucked blood
and gave me life.

Now this
womb-toad
kicks in my belly,
a moon unravelling
for different answers.
I see an old eye
in the unborn brain
eroding a wilderness
confined to my memory.

I see the new moon
swollen from
sores,
sullen and
decomposing
in a body
arisen from death.

What are you
because I must live
wanting you?
It's hard to refuse
happiness
when love is the only
alternative.

The Pact

I tried to touch you
with my eyes closed
and felt you waver,
uncertain as ice.

I heard
ice-worms
drowning in your
body, multiplying
in dead numbers.

I think of you often
this way in winter,
needing some immeasurable grief
to carry me through
the season.

I think of you
in the forest,
in the deep snow
making tracks that imagine
no betrayer.

I know you.
I *am* the forest;
my deep scent reels
against the dark.

I unfold
like darkness
and you are lost in me.

Once I discovered
a wounded deer.
Convinced of hunger
I ate its heart.

You know
if I found you dying
I would do the same.

Night Wind

Somewhere out there
we are animals—
in the cold wind always
blowing from death,
breathing its
storm under my
dry skin,
beating bone-music
into the tight black drum
of my fear.

Wind cast us
in all directions—
my face collapsed
in your eyes,
pieces of your heart
came away in my hands.
I felt some strange cold
distance of touch
in your body I've entered
a hundred times.

Wind gives
no reason for taking,
only tears at the
blind window
as I lie
silent against you.

Against you.
Our bodies know
what the silence is.

The sound has
no ending, like a dream
you never return
to. I still remember
that emptiness—
the first whisper
of darkness and the dead wind rising
all night.

Ghost Words

I should be buried
like a seed
absorbed in
dreaming,
drifting
between senses
like a cold sleep reaching
to drown the
dreamer.

My grave-clothes should be
plain
like birds on a
flat lake,
like trees in winter.

My grave would be
shallow—
each hour I will become
more like air.
Blood will be
darkness and
darkness is a stone
without centre.

My face will be
beautiful—
haunted into flight
like a frightened
animal,
nameless and
broken
without a shadow.

Say you know
my face,
shape without
centre or
shadow.
Death is not
silence
but the echo of
all sound.

My body smells of
this, of dead and
dying animals.
I only believed in silence
when you would
listen to me.

Making Blood

We are
dancing

we are
making blood

our bodies
disguise the
dance
where love is
impossible to
hide.

We know
the way,
the memory's
bone-music

our bodies
enter the dance

we are
making
each other

out of
visions,
out of
old photographs

we are dancing

out of the words
we have spoken
for other people

out of the
long silence

we are
breaking

into the dance
that is the
real bond

we are making
animal blood.

Today

I saw our ghosts
making love under
the trees.

Your ghost was a
dark tide
rising to
flood the earth.

My ghost
started crying:
the future seemed
so predictable.

As I Go

In winter
the mountain makes
a woman's face
crying out
after each man
she remembers.

In springtime
she is
steep shadowy
silence,
patient
as the moon's
surface.

I wore her
shadow
like the
skeleton of a
fish,
lured into
deep certainties,
easily betrayed.

Wanting you
I feel like this
mountain
any season

I mean
worn down
wearing
out of the earth's
innocence

knowing you

needing.

Possessions

Seanach
of hosts

black gatherer

toad of the
wound I say
my prayers about

lie down and be
little

forgive me
an old woman
sagging against
lies

Seanach
element I
warm to
brush the blood
from my womb
without ceremony
open the
morning mail
without certainty

Seanach
I see the
pity
the faith that makes you
animal

my animal
waking to my
nights' hunger
stroking my
fatal hunger

wanting
without desire

Seanach
you are lost
you are unable
to sleep as
I alone
inhabit
the dark

Seanach
you dream of a
lost familiar

needing darkness
that moves around you
like weather
with no
discipline

but awkwardly
triumphant

Seanach
I am not sure
of anything
indistinct as
pleasure

I've seen
your skull
and will always
remember it

perhaps you've
held mine
in your
long white hands

Seanach
go down
sink to
human will
forget
for a moment
what strength is

perhaps it will help you
sleep

Seanach
when I am
old
be compassionate

remember me
as a
woman
an idea without children
to learn by

remember
what choice means
and how few of us ever
needed to be
happy

A Life

You are locked
into darkness
like the memory of a
whale

clenched
like winter
in the grip of
dying flowers.

I enter you
like a trap
half-sprung by my
curious shadow.
I enter you
like a grave
in a dream of
growing dead.

You are locked
into this
dream
below surfaces of
sleep

waking
in the whale's
belly
bleeding the whale's
blood.

You are locked
in a life
you have chosen
to remember:

at the moment of
dying
no choices are
good.

Habit

I have dreamed about
this place before;
alone all the
long winter
with sadness like
gunfire
declaring its own
course.

We lie
together
close in the same
memory.
It is the guns
that frighten you
but I am afraid
of the silence.

We have been here
before—
our bodies
remember this.
The death that does not
disturb us now
settles like a
new grave
behind your smile.

We wait for it,
counting backward
from the first
moment—
admitting the end
before moving on
like ghosts into the dust

of our own nameless
shadows.

You hold my hand
like the wing of a
wounded bird.
Snow covers
the silence; in my dream
we are finally
waking.

I tell you
I am afraid of
pain
now that the silence
is over.

I hear you offer
that final weapon

believing it is yours.

Chiaroscuro

How could I live
south of anywhere—
the wind has come to
know me,
"part-blood" the sea
calls me.

Do I keep moving north
beyond object or
direction? Is distance
measured by
confusion? I hate
to leave a place

unaltered; something
must stay
to complete the vision.

You love the sun;
for you the world
is never a problem.
When your bones are
covered with dust
mine will be moss.
I could not rest
under the cramped earth.

I would die here
like a stone stopped
breathing—
I will wait
for fungus to
close me.

You love the heat:
we will not die
together.

I resist thinking about you
somewhere alone in the
shadows

It is the thirst I
worry about,
the drowning without
water.

The Right Word
for Seán

i

The silence you
filled me with
is a dream I
cannot remember

nothing
replaces you

not even
the silence.

ii

The words
I once spoke for you
have vanished

memories
like caves
are filled with the
dead bones of
things.

Among them
your skeleton
heavy with sleep.

The words
I tried to
wake you with
is the reason
you are smiling.

iii

In a dream
you stand over my grave
trying to find the right word
to end the funeral.

It's strange
since I haven't died
and I can't seem to make you
believe that.

You stand
looking uncomfortable
holding my old
umbrella.
I get the feeling
you know how
the dream ended.

iv

When this photograph
was taken
were you thinking about
death?
What thought is frozen
that only begins to thaw
in time and through
constant exposure?

You *look* dead
only your eyes moved
at the last moment.

Maybe you thought
about me.

v

Because the wolves
smell you
your dream won't
save us

it only puts words
between silence
and death.

Your silence
is no answer
until I can hear it

as long as
you pretend to sleep
I won't wake you.

Parting Ways

There are signs
everywhere
each time the moon sheds her
dull feathers
each time
something dies.

There are signs
in cobwebs
woven across
cold water,
there are messages
in blood.

You know them
for death is the same

in all languages.
Death shames the body
with no voice
to carry the blame.

Only the blind
can see through
memory:
I believe in signs.

Only the dead
can lead you to the
beginning
or leave you at the
crossroads
scribbling in their dust.

Sea Change

Off shore
the fish thread
like lures through the
waterweed.
We don't
know each other.

A lunar wraith,
the moon rose for me.
I regretted the
dark sea,
the wreathed birds
riding outward on the wind.

I've watched birds
before this
on other beaches—

I've seen the tide
make a ghost of the moon.

I gave the world up:
the sea claimed me.
Half fish I breathed
in uncertain water.

I trusted no one,
living again
in the cool depth of
mirrors, turning against fate
in the windy gulfs.

I needed to
touch you, to feel
a fixed skin. My eyes stopped
at stone, closed like a
drowned man.

It was
only beginning.
Half blinded I came
wrecked out of the
sea, no fish at all
but weathered and cold.

You were there
to meet me. Each day
you concealed more, knew
less of me. My eyes fed
and became strong.

I had you then.
No doubt all journeys
end this way,
drifting inland under
a dry moon, regardless
of tides.

The Wolf

I killed a
wolf
but I knew
he wasn't
dying.

He spoke to me—
it wasn't you
but the voices
came from you.

I can't remember
the words he used,
if they *were* words
or just wounds
closing.

I laid him down
under the dark trees.
I listened for his
breath.

I was waiting for the sign
that I would
know you by,
watching for the eyes
that say
you remember.

It seemed to me
that the wolf was
smiling

(how can I be sure)

it looked like
the last smile
you gave me

as I walked out of
that forest
and into another story.

II. Recovery

O and a gash...
—John Berryman

The Child Js Father of the Man

The rat has been dead
under the sink for
three days.

You poisoned
it.
It died
while we were
making love
one night

when the baby
is born
I will still be
indifferent.

All Will Fall

Old murderer
mother

how they
pluck you.
Drink on
little ones,
suck up blood and
die.

You'll get
as good as you
give:
you always gave me
nothing.

I was born with
witch power and
two wings.
Somebody cut
them off.

I accuse
even the noblest of
men. I accuse
the priests and the
women of
holy darkness.

I want them to
burn forever
like my wings that were burned
for evil.

I'll suck on the
blood of that
murdering
father; his old wig
is crawling with
worms

his old cock
is no good for a
maggot.

That's why
I don't give anything
either.

I just crawl
out of the ash
I just wish
my ribs were wings.

"The Babies Are Growing into Their Suits"

I could see them
being hatched from their
tombs like
fish—
dribbling with
salt eyes and
sudden human lips.

Some carried flags,
others stiffened like
old citizens
scattering newspapers and
cigarettes under the
blind issueless
statues.

Some grew
stubble on their
chins, perished behind
beards. Others
preferred masks.

I could see them
like defeated ghosts
entering the grave,
nurse-like and
efficient
rattling the friendly bars.

No womb
nourished them,
the born-to-die
babies. No seed
sent a possible messenger,
no vague talk
hustled the cells to
mesh.

Something else
could do it
better: some
intractable marriage,
tube-like and
convulsing

some bright
baby seed
swaddled in the
dark cupboard.

I could hear them
in the nursery
planning their
stranglehold.
I knew better than to
face their infantry.

The father trims his
moustache, more or
less survives. The

breathing mother
has no other memory:
she understands
her weapon.

Afterthought

i

Seed
don't swim into
anything but
space
I want
enormous darkness
inside me,
unnatural
emptiness,
not small fingers and
bodies all lodged and
lost, all growing up
into the impossible
accident of
existence—all
assuming names
and later on
having feelings.

Seed
stop at the first sign of
discovery
I don't want a
circus or
enormous responsibility
I don't want
intruders or
burrowers or

anything my own shape
can't define.

Turn back
before darkness
blinds you, don't let
the pale and
shaky
tempt you.
Don't fumble
when you sense the
bars, don't feed
anything too
fierce.

ii

My godmother is
wise—she
dazzles me! Like you
she appears
suddenly and
smiles, wearing
a grey suit, and
says, quite
defenceless,
she can't foresee
anything.

Don't go,
she says,
if the gates
are closed. Never
love an
audience, don't marry
an animal trainer.

iii

Seed
I don't want you swigging
my cool
statistical juices
though I don't expect
a fair execution.

So
be disciplined—
don't stretch
or sink,
don't labour with the moon.

You pump
inside my breast
to the music of
blood

your bones crack
like bells
to feed the heart alive.

All Deceive

Your first wife
gave you a
child—
your second wife
the promise of
another.

I only offered
the bones of a
dying animal.

Beware
of your children
bound together
by blood.

Be careful
of the skeleton
held together
by dust.

The Frog

i

I thought her body
was a frozen tree

I was supposed to
wake up one day
and find myself
thawed in her branches.

Instead I made
enemies of men
I made ghosts
out of
happy women.

I decided
never to be
born again
but grew up
so lonely
I couldn't sleep
without light.

ii

It's a frog
who is
eating her,
small girl alone
in a small
boat

she is
sad
but the frog is
hungry

she is
lonely
though the frog has
a human face.

iii

In the morning
the boat
will be a
bird

a small girl
with unsteadying
branches.

She will drift
into my heart
and sleep
like an old
woman.

Eventually
she will
die there

in spite of my breathing.

iv

Moon bone whistling
in the frozen tree

the children have
other names
for you

deceit
deceive

moon-circus
in their
curious eyes

moon-frog
spits the
moon-flies

she's making
witch-evil
to keep me alive

she's dreaming
the right lies
to wake me.

Vampires Should Be Liberated

I think
vampires should be
liberated—
tended like
war memorials.

As a group they should win
the Nobel Prize for
peace.

Nobody likes
failures—
it's all right to
die but don't
disappoint anyone.
It's easy to laugh—
vasectomies make sense
after all.

Equal rights
for vampires—
slave labour must
end. Free blood
for nursing
mothers, compulsory
dental care.

Relax.
It's simple.
Dying is a free
experience—
enjoy.
If the teeth fit,
bite it. Ignore the
politicians—they're bound
to take death
seriously.

Consummation

Happy Birthday
Skull
I hope you're

happy now
they've even named a
constellation after you.
They could see it
at night
through their
high-powered
telescopes;
they say you can
predict the future.

Happy Nothingness
Skull
when I was small
I believed in
imaginings.
I used to be afraid
of bones—
they were calm
and invisible
where blood was
easily proven.

In photographs
my skin sheltered you;
even then
you had the look of a
prisoner.
If I were you
I would welcome the
chance. There are
worse things yet
than survival.

Sometimes I see
light and
forget your
nearness.

The casual way
you erase the past:
"Knock Knock"
"Who's there?"
"Is a skull necessary on a..."

Merry Merry
Meaningless Mess
when I was small
I remember being
untouched by you.
I made
seed cakes
out of poisonous grass.
I was
skinny then
and hardly aware of flesh.

Happy Someday
Skull
I'd choose other holes
for my eyes if I
didn't know you
would be suspicious.
I think we may become
good friends
one day

in the meantime
you may well
outlive me.

Recovery

Frances, I've
idolized you
too far. All I've known

is blackness; I can't
find remedies
anywhere.

I've prepared to
leave you—the nurse
talks of weakness and a
pure heart—the judge
still puzzles me—he must be
terribly lonely.

Remember taking off your
clothes in the
woods—goddamn
it makes me feel
desperate, you were so
tight.

Your father builds
bridges—some of them
collapse. A nasty
coincidence—I was
halfway across.

You would be pleased
with me, Frances,
I'm learning to
hold my spoon. I will eat
someday and draw lines
on paper. I could probably learn
to write some stuff.

I don't believe
you won't listen
or answer some of my
letters; I can't
climb out of bed
without remembering

the secret you cut
in on.

I want you to be
honest: have these
last years
been difficult?

Draw the curtains,
I'm in two films
today.
The director said
it's a
sure cure—there's a
warrant out for my
health.

After a whole life of
needles and
mess I'm a
whore tonight
in the
puppet show.
Professional or
otherwise
I'm everybody's
latest hero.

I'm famous
everywhere but
Frances it's
miserable. I'm appearing
tomorrow again
if you want me—
the future begins
at dusk.

Juggernaut

I wrote myself a
letter—it
began: *thousands*
of us were
given mercilessly
oh god I haven't been
in such nervous
company for
ages. After all
it's just fragments—
I find I'm
worn out
and quite inadequate
to continue.

One of us got
so cold he
fell in the lake.
Drowned, poor
bastard—
he's dead.
Grandmother writes:
The lilac is in
bloom and all is
splendid. When are you
coming here for
tea?

What is left
that is tireless and still
believable?
I'm more or less
destroyed—I didn't
fit in anywhere. Even my
long legs

weren't athletic;
cake decorations
are always for the first
moment.

Grandmother was flustered
when I was born:
a first girl!
Days later
there were six more.
Grandfather knew better,
the emphasis on
important matters.
A girl can't be
a politician—he was
disappointed about the
Common Market.

It's all
unrelated, I wrote
later. Looks and
impulses: I left
the locked ward and became
nauseated.

Grandmother writes:
It's beastly hot—
please come.
The incinerator covers the
ground with ash—
tea's on the
juggernaut
at half past five.

A Private Joke
for Al Purdy

Write about all the
horrors, an American
tells me
on an unmapped
street corner
in Mexico City
handing out invitations
to a flowing
existential experience.
I lie about
who I am. I don't
want to write anything
about Mexico.

And turn away.
*Hey, Canada, come back
and talk.*

I think of
Al and Eurithe at
a party in
Progreso. Al got
drunk and left his
bathing suit behind.
Could have happened
to anyone.
The cook passed out
on the floor (broken dishes,
delusions, etc.). It couldn't
have happened
anywhere.

The American wants
statistics. He wants

to meet later—to
communicate openly.
I agree and
lie about my address.

And take a direct flight
to Vancouver
in the morning,
sitting next to a
doctor who tells me
women bleed longer
in Mexico.

The Impstone
for Roy Kiyooka and Daphne Marlatt

i

The day the man
stumbled and
cursed the stone's
existence

the stone created
woman
out of another stone.

Darkness fell
like a thick velvet
curtain over the
land. The stone saw
that it was good.

And on the seventh day
he rested.

ii

This stone has been
rained on
this stone has been
left out in the
dark.

This stone has been
stepped on
though it never hurt
anyone.

Pick up the stone—
you will notice these
scars.
Drop it again
it won't blame you.

iii

This stone
is the guilt
each person takes
upon him;

this stone
is a
mass-murderer,
a poet,
a thief.

This stone is a
god, a
failure, a
government.

This stone
stands for

nothing—
it has
no country.

iv

This stone
was an island
once;
tourists would take
picnics to its
beaches;
fishermen would take
shelter in its
coves.

The stone knew
what it felt like
to be sinking.
Some people
changed the
island's name
in memory of a
dead politician.

v

In your house
nobody mentions
this stone.
It is asleep
beside the fireplace,
it is dreaming
of warmth.

Nobody mentions it
because they are
frightened.

Nobody feels it
because they are
cold.

One night
it changes
into an apparition.

Nobody knows why.

Your house trembles
like an animal dying.
It sees its reflection
for the first time.

vi

This stone
knows what it's like
to be chipped away
into nothing

to be blown up
into pieces
to make roads for people
to walk down
complaining all the
way.

This stone should have been
a writer
knowing the truth's disguised
as a bulldozer or a
typewriter

knowing the devil is
always present
wearing a
white carnation

being sucked like a
cigar

until he succeeds.

vii

This stone is
everybody's
culture hero.
He has been made to
explain his dream
once too often.

His dream
is the same scene
over and over.
He is standing with a
loaded gun in his
mouth
trying to explain
his feelings.

Bandicoot

My house is
alone in me;
I appear on
country beaches,
in old photographs
nobody won
prizes for.

I gloat like a
woman insanely
pregnant with the
whole militia behind her.

I'm jealous of how it
happened.

It's a question of
career:
how to say
I need you
when nerve gas is so
lethal and
Biafra is everywhere
these days.

My house is
safe in me;
worlds unhinge like
lost constellations.
I've left
most of my friends—
I confess it seemed
natural.

I don't know
how it happened
but I also appeared at the
Resurrection.
I saw
John Berryman
there
eating an apple.

Like bandicoot,
he kept saying,
I have this insatiable
point of view.

III. Success Story

Please die, I said
so I can write about it.
  —Margaret Atwood

Day of Reckoning
for David

This morning
the horizon was not
there; I saw a
forest shrivelled
where you had slept
with your twigs of
memory, dry
leaves.

There was no movement,
only the ghost of a
shadow too dead for
seeing
and you
struggling like a
crowded room to
recover silence.

Your mirror world reflects
your own darkness:
how am I to see?
I witness the world's
conscience—let it all
go by. Somehow we survive
like missing people
though who is to say
where the sea is
without water?

Last night
a dream racked your
vision—this morning
you arrived with a new
finality. You were here
before the dawn reached us—
I heard the day crack
like barriers against fate.

I said
let the world contain
its own madness
or else go down.
It is hard to rest,
you told me,
with so many lives in danger.

But are you really
safer than I am
or does caring lead you
nearer to destruction?

                    I heard
voices in the garden
calling for you—people
trampling over the last days
and all things that grow
for no reason.

What Happens to the Carcass

No
animal sound
no more
old woman
sound

no fangs
bared on the
staircase leaping
up

no more enemies at
windows
glaring into the
dense fact of
darkness.

It's gone and
you're gone.
I see it.
Like a point of
light
vanishing
vanishing
you have dressed up
to go, you have
walked out only
a daredevil with
fire on his side.

Last time the flame spat
you reached out, withdrawn
into ritual. I had
to wait till your
face reentered:
you piled bones
into the ash
and crouched all night
like a cracked shell.

So walk the
tightrope
swing with the
creaky birds and

flowers I don't
think your
Indian magic
works.

Your secrets
burned out;
no paralysis
needs defining.
It is your will
to remain alone.

So belong to
yourself
and to no other:
there is no way
to change, no hope
as wild.

Ant Doom

The first night
I left
offerings:
thin slices of
bread
and a tablespoon
of preserves.

They followed the
crumb trail out
before morning;
by the second night
they trusted me.

I left
honey and

oatcakes
to urge them
from their corners.

They were
grateful
as guests
should be
and I,
as a host,
made them feel
welcome.

When I brought *you* home
you had
different ideas.
Watching things die
for you
was entertainment.

And when I
wasn't looking
you sprinkled some
white powder
"painless and
instant"
with the ease of a
magician

you who knew nothing about
magic
or how long it takes
a spirit to die.

"It Is a True Error to Marry with Poets"

Words by themselves
are like
dead-end streets.
You can choose either
death
or infinite regression.

I chose
you.
You recovered.

You're a
wary traveller
preferring back roads
to illusion.
I pass everywhere,
believing in signs.

You write like you
talk
dedicating each poem
to safety at a
reasonable distance.
*For chrissake I could
get drunk
and write poetry too.*

We accuse each other
of repetition;
I've memorized all the
lies.

Truth's a
refutable vulture:

we've failed the test
of time.

"It's Hard to Be Kind to a Cannibal"

You're killing me
I said
still hoping for
second chances.

I love you
you answered
believing in
lost causes.

I'll miss you
I said
still caring about
reasons. The story needs
thickening. Pass
the blood.

It's easy:
you need me
anyway. I feel like a
feast—we have
too much in common.

You ask me for a
quick meal;
I leave early.
It's wrong to die
on a full stomach.

Two Minutes for Hooking

i

You are leaving.

I have just shown you
my collection of
masks.

You kiss me goodbye
but your face is
trembling.

The masks look like
bad imitations of
you

before you became
my lover.

ii

You are leaving.

Outside
you play a
trumpet solo
to a herd of
starving cattle.

I can hear you
from my window
where I wait with my
broken xylophone.

Your wife
is an heiress
from an old
military family.

The only
military music
I know
is the kind that they play
at funerals.

iii

You are leaving.

My heart feels like
a shivering egg
that some
wild bird
has abandoned.

You like the
image
but it's too much
responsibility.

What do you
expect
on an island
as small as this?

iv

You are leaving.

First we make love
perfecting
habitual patterns.

A photographer
is waiting
at the end of the
bed.

You take her arm
and smile
professionally.

You don't even hear
the applause.

v

You are leaving.

Already I have
forgotten your
smile.

I think you must make
other people
happy

other people whose scars
are still a
mystery.

Literary Evening

I don't need to know
what book clubs
you belong to,
how you celebrate your
birthdays or
how you got famous.
Don't you see

I'm inflatable
and I need a good
punching bag
to keep me company.

I wonder about your new
belts-and-chain
method; you've got me
nailed. I'm not
a coffin substitute
and thinking just gets me
furious.

So you see how
it is—I'm
not at home
most days. It's hard
to be the wife of a
critic;
I'd rather be
bored by a poet.

O Grave
Where Js Thy
Victory
I Corinthians xv.55

Yesterday
I loved you
today well
I don't know
death never
hesitates
death wants to
get married.
Death does not
eat properly

death believes in
civilization
death drinks
beer
death watches
hockey
death is
invincible
death is always
happy.
Yesterday I
loved you
well today I don't
know
death has
false teeth
death has
bad habits
death makes me
furious
death is
possessive
germs feed on
death but
death doesn't
know that.
Yesterday
well I think
I loved you
but now I
just don't know
death wants me
to live with him
death would make life
impossible
death wants to
meet my family
death wants

babies
death believes
true love is
eternal
death depends on things being
finished.
I don't think
death knows himself
death is,
after all,
only human.

Success Story

You're full of
surprises
these days
in your
lime-green
niceties and your
flash irresistible
stock.

Besides that
you're good at
it. I could
of course
take no interest
but I like your
sentence structures.

I guess zero's
a good number:
anyway
you made it.
So much for the
gobbledygook

I can't spare any
autographs this week.

I've written about you
to friends you'll
never meet: you are
too busy
inventing them.
I've told them you don't
deserve any of it;
I have to write a book
where you are the
unfortunate ending.

IV. Archaeologists and Grave Robbers

No, children, grave robbers
and archaeologists
are as different as
night and day—
which is when they work.
—John Corsiglia

Mourning Song

My great-grandmother
was dying.
They left her
for wolves,
vanished like
worms into the
taut black carcass
of the night.

She wanted it that way.

> *The white hollow bone*
> *speaks through me.*

She left me her
memory, who wouldn't love
this country now.
She gave me back my name.

My skin is
paler than hers—
I have a feeling
she sees that.

My grandmother married
a city man:
I get this feeling
she's forgiven that.

My great-grandmother
is alive in me—
she calls me to her own.
The old frog-moon
lays her eggs in my heart.

> *The white hollow bone*
> *bleeds through me.*

Elegy

I go along alone above
the shore,
half-spirit
older than that
sometimes.
The sea is the

coffin house of
frogs,
dark waterweed graveyard
pulled from the moon's
direction.

I never knew loss
till the sea gave way
under me;
the black mooring of
ghosts
wrenched and the tide
slipped empty.

All night they
stormed the beaches
listening
for a sign

familiar ghosts
of elements air and
water.

      A frog grew frail
      under his thin mask
      shivering when their fingers
      crushed him
      cruel as the depth of
      currents.

I cursed those
dark gods
the long night endless
with no sound.

I cursed the closed eyes,
the human lips

forgetting the songs
frogs sing
on the burial of
another.

     This frog sleeps
     avenged
     by the moon's silence

     shadow out of that
     silence

     surviving
     even death.

Against
kuganaa...black magic...
rats inside...

Up past the Indian graveyard
the sea has
uprooted trees.
The dead dream of
nets flashing,
clutch against
kuganaa—
dark magic in a
dying tongue.

I dig for a
darker stone,
the kind
rats are afraid of.
Black and silvery
to keep out evil,
I pick away the
mirror-flakes

to hold against
kuganaa.

The beach scuttles
from under me,
drags its
shell-hoard from the
strain of tides.
I hear rats
waking in the
graveyard,
growing fat by the
memorial.
Rats giving birth
under the long grass.

I cross the old bridge
by daylight
avoiding their eyes.
I move
without seeing
into the tall cedars,
far past the
dead flowers.

I slip like a memory
following the dark
road

my white skin has
fooled them
every time.

Shadow-Shamans

(Koyah the Raven and Ninstints of the Eagle Crest were two powerful
Haida chiefs during the 1800s. They lived on Skang'wai or Red Cod Island
off the southwest coast of the Queen Charlotte Islands, or Haida Gwaii.)

Their bones sleep
in the forest
fallen behind the
rain-wall.
I heard laughter
and a
ghost-raven:
his skin was like a
pale sea-flower.

I heard it was
Koyah,
chief of
Raven-town.
He told me
this story:

*Skulkinance was a great chief who had
two sons. These were called Koh and
Skindaskun. They lived in the village
called Qadadjans where everyone was
always talking.*
*Skulkinance was returning to his village
with his two sons. They had been hunting
for seals up the coast.*
*They stopped at night to make a fire and
cook some devil-fish. Skulkinance felt
the presence of enemies.*
*"Koh," he said, addressing his eldest son,
"go to the canoe and get me my harpoon."*
Koh replied that he had no use for it and

besides that he was too hungry.
"Skindaskun," he said, addressing his
younger son, "go to the canoe and get me
my harpoon." Skindaskun replied that he
had no use for it and besides he was too
sleepy.
Skulkinance addressed each of his sons a
second time.
Again they disobeyed him.
Then Skulkinance jumped up, ran down to
the canoe, climbed in and pushed himself
far out to sea.
He looked back over his shoulder and saw
his sons lying with their throats cut
open. In the firelight he could see an
arm of the devil-fish they had just eaten
reaching out of their throats.

I saw
armbones in the
rock-pools,
heard thunder
in the dark.

I saw it was
Ninstints,
chief of the
Eagles.
He told me
this story:

Once I was nobody.
I went to the top of a mountain and
stayed there for a long time. I ate
devil's club. I ate whatever I could find.
I wanted to know what my name would be.
Then I came down from the mountain and I
was sick for a long time. The shaman sang
for me and I opened my mouth to tell him

what I had seen. Some rats just came
running out of my stomach. The last one
to run out of me was white.
The people in the village gathered there
to see it. "Give me back my own," I cried
to them. The last one to come out of me
meant that I had eaten a small spirit.
Then I was somebody.
My people called me a chief and
told me what my name would be.
My people called me their chief,
He-who-is-equal-to-two.

I found
rain-stones
under the
tree roots,
fire-pits in the
ghost-lodge.

I went to sleep
in a nest of
ravens
but woke up holding
the claw of an
eagle.

Archaeologists and Grave Robbers

When they dug you
out, the earth
wrenched. Your fate
was like a
grave-image,
weird and
shadowy, rooted
to define your
place.

Your skull hoarded
its loss: handfuls
of red seeds.
Too deep
to be uncovered,
too closed
for solitary reasons—
only the eyes
kept watch.

Old woman-witch,
they opened you.
Your secrets
fell out,
forever out,
into that silence.

They wanted to
reach you—
to label the
blank times.
For all your dead
each seed is
counted;
too many
to gather,
too little
to leave behind.

Skookumchuk
for Tom York

I guess it's in
my blood
to want to be like
Emily Carr. I don't know
much about her

but we've been to
some of the same
places.

The north is
the end for me—
I'm in love with a
man I'll never
meet.
Indian Jimmy from
Nanootkish (was there ever
such a place?).

Emily and I
shared him for a while—
I know that. He was
impossible to paint
and what's more
she found the forest
a deeper attraction.

*The eagle
eats the land,*
I write in my
journal. A nurse
wraps my wrists and
says next time
don't use
third-rate machinery.

*Give me back
my own:*
I want to go where
Ninstints found his
name.
Jimmy rows
further into the
sea-drift

Emily says
it's too rough
to go sailing.

She paints
the unexposed skin,
the masks behind
loss. My notebooks
have been empty
up until now;
I write often to
Nanootkish
but my letters
always
come back.

Kung

Village of the
moon, of the
small night

I name you now
what others have
lied about.

Even the dead
have abandoned you,
floating deep
down, deep
beyond stillness.

You possess me,
a spirit no wilder
than my own, no
less hungry—
you haunt me.

I felt your hammer
in the dry wood
chipping my shape.
I killed a
devil-fish;
the sea stank
and swallowed me.

I saw you watching
from the root-caves
old and beyond
injury. You must have known
I could never leave.

The place reminds me of
death, of waiting
on the last edges.
The stones are
faceless; the trees,
empty.

Village of
hushed voices,
your soul is
trapped.

Your secrets drowned
with me
though my shadow walks
on the last shore.

Lure

Raven
in the rain binds
silence and
cedar

one part
feather
four parts
bone.

In the wind
he weaves
cedar-bark,
swallows
the sun

he asks words
to feather the
dry throat
a song to spin
silence into
blood.

In the rain
he carves the
bone hollow
to help blow sickness
out.

Raven
hears the moon,
the tired heart
of cedar

he follows the
frog-echo
under a low bank.

Raven beats
his spirit-drum,
taps for his
spirit-helper.

Salmon rises
to cedar
on wind
under dark water

river rises
to roots
and the echo of rain.

Dead Eagle

The beach gave nothing
but signs of what
the mist had been

where it hung
too lightly to the
whore-sea
shrinking
to hoard its own.

I could see your face
like a pit on the
earth's skin,
sun-ridged as the
earth's core
where your eyes had strained
to reason with light.

Your hands were hooked
to wings
unable to grip.
Your skull made a bone sheath
for the wind.

I watched
with the patience of
moss, forgetting

the sea's unrest.
The forest kept its
own secret
far from the snares of
others.

The skin you wore
was a way learned:
let the scald-crow suck
a miser-teat;
forgive the mind its
dull damage.
Your claws stayed to
tear, undisguised
by words

the skin has its
own version:
clench of
dead meat lying.

Yatza

I'd say that
seaweed is where
you came from:
long green
waterweed
person, kelp-brother
to the codfish
turned
belly-up.

I'd say your grandfathers
were birds
who flew out of
darkness.

Their bones mark
the channel now—
you can see them if you wait
for low water.

I'd say your father was an
eagle—chipped a raven
out of stone. She
was your mother.
Your sisters scuttled like
giant crabs from her
womb, but you swam
like an otter from the
sea-egg that was
you.

Black-eyed,
scaly, darker than
the rest—she knew
water was your
element. Each day
the tides shift but you are
calm and unchangeable.

Someday they'll
bury you
all wrapped in
cedar-bark—sea-warped
and tangled with the
weed. You'll
sink like a
bone to a
similar fate,
your hair wound up
and your eyes tight.

I'd say they'll wait
for you, for the
beak of the night to

open. They'll hear your
voice on the
turning tide.

I'd say you'd surface
when the moon was
new, rising
like a whale out of
nowhere
and then sounding
the closed waters.

Kaisun

An eagle fed you on eyes
all winter long,
brought favours
to your door.
The ghosts rattled
the grave-box walls.

Your smile tightened
like an old woman's fist,
your face relaxed.
Crows entered
your dry heart
picking up scraps
from the raven's cache.

All winter
your blood ran,
you were present
in every house.
Your voice ruled the
bright hearth,
your spirit sang
in the dancer's mask.

240

Haliotis dugong
mask-spirit and skin
bursting the toad-skulls
open, stiffening
in the wind.

All winter the women
came to you,
crouched to your
new heat.
Each night your
demon entered—
moaned like a
flower blooming and
died before morning.

Your spirit was
naked, went for
fish off the
rock-shelves.
Prophecy gave you
shelter; you saw
devils behind the mask.

Your new ring
wrenched like the
moon: iron praised your
finger's hand.
You fasted for
days and your visions
became clear; drums
told of sadness, how
the village would be
lost.

Haliotis dugong
iron-sadness and drum
sucking the fish-lips
open, stiffening
in the sun.

Now the ravens
taunt you, the
eagles hunt on a
different shore. Your
bones lie open
in the half-light,
your skull is troubled
by an unremembered dream.

Ghost Song

Whale in the
water is like
dead men wading.
Bone pierces the
spirit-belly,
looks like
tentacles rising.

I am afraid of the
moon
in the dark night
shining.
The trees look like
mountains,
their shadows hang
like hair.

Whale makes a
human sound,
voice of an old man
dying.

He opens his mouth up,
looks like a
devil feeding.

I was a
whale once
but then I had a
bird's shadow.
A devil breathed his
breath in me,
turned feathers into
fins.

Whale in his sleep
is like dead men
dreaming.
Darkness makes him
look like a frog;
he needs many faces
to keep the dead from waking.

Once I had a
whale's shape
but then I had only
sadness.
A devil sucked my
spirit out;
now I am a ghost
wading inland to die.

Jnvocation

Listen.
It is too late
for sleep;
nothing escapes
the conscience of the

damned. Listen.
There is no reason
for pain—Pain began
when life
ceased.

I draw you in.
I wait.

One by one
the animals are
leaving.
When they go
it is something I see:
there are no
choices.

The animals have slept
too long, have
listened
too closely. They
creep away,
their wounds like
bridges from one past
over another.

The animals know
safety is a
fool's heaven,
forests
are for dying in.

My grey ones,
my broken ones,
stealth is no
virtue when it comes to
being lost.

I know you are
happy
I know your bones are
sacred.

Listen.
It is too late for
anything;
I cannot provide for
more.

I wait.
I wonder.

What secrets do you have
to surrender;
where do you go
that it is
forever?

Firebrand

I saw the moon
burst like a
puffball from the
stabbed body of the
trees. I imagined
the caught animals—
my familiar among them.

No one would be
saved—I remembered
the vacuum below me,
the stick-house city
burning outward toward
water.

I stepped between
logs—drowned the way
a stone does
forgetful of surfaces
unaltered and
falling endlessly.

Then you—
my familiar—
in one disguise
I'm not sure of.
You are so beautiful
I'd always want
to have you near me.

I remembered
fire; the cold slit of your
tongue opened an
old wound. You drew
your kisses in,
buried yourself in a
new armour.

The fire took everything.
I'm more alone now
than ever.

I dreamed your name
over and over
thinking it might bring you
near.

I heard nothing
but the sound of my own
calling

my familiar
my own
close your eyes down
over me.

The Carver

Time is a
beggarman,
rats hang on his
heart.

Waves break
over his heart,
seconds waste
like old weapons.

Crows nest in his heart.

On his breath
a great lock
is chained to a
plough.

Poverty is a
good business now
and again. He no longer
works in stone.

Metals are clearer,
bone is nearer,
but wood understands:

Time mainly fashions neglect.

Becky Swan's Book
1977

Elisa and Mary

Currant bread, simnel cake and
coloured eggs were eaten on the
picnic. Oh, it was a good
picnic, an elegant one.

We spread the ground with food
for the beautiful women.
Elisa and Mary were joined together
at the hip and shoulder—they were
born that way—joined—but we decided
to let them come on our picnic.

I would not want to be born joined

promise me I will not be born joined to anyone.

It Is Wrong

Mary Matlin
why do you poison her?
Why do you not pity her,
she who is crying out, "Help, help!"

Rebecca Perigo is one of your
gullible customers.
You should not make her drink,
not when the cup is bottomless.

Especially This One

I have seen Edric's body
devoured by hounds
and Edona in the forest
convulsed with laughter.

She kissed a one-legged soldier.
She drank mead with a well-known robber.

Ah, but some women like that are
wicked. Some women are wicked.

Known for Their Bones

Lucy Littlecote
wearing 18th-century boots
was found bricked up in the
rectory only yesterday.

Dame Phillips
took her there.

Both skeletons were found the
same way, dressed up in
wedding clothes.

They were playing hide-and-go-seek
evidently.

Lady Eleanor

Lady Eleanor sold her soul,
received a prayer book from the vicar.

Her body was delivered from torment,
delivered from demonry.

Her cold body was placed on the altar,
received a colder kiss from the verger.

Or Worse

Grand Albert,
fat mad dog,
made love to a witch,
made love to a carrion crow.

He did not know; he did not recognize her
for she was an old artist.

She stuck three thorns in his fat
dog's heart, infested his neighbours.

Sometimes their thumbs ought to be
torn off—witches who do such things as
killing people and infesting neighbours.

Who Can Be Trusted

Monkey-face, Old Mace,
is a poacher. I know, I know,
he is a respectable clergyman
but I've seen him fetch a club after our
father's sheep on more than one occasion.

I've seen him in the wolf pits bandying.
He gave arsenic to Mistress Blandy.

He said she was loose of tongue but it
wasn't true, she came from a very religious
family.

God will suck the bad ones up,
God snatches the bad ones.

Still They Call It Marriage

Mother wanted me to marry—
she brought me a red-headed man,
she brought me a holy man.

I let down my hair.
I confessed to uttering spells.
Mother brought me an organ grinder
who married me thinking I had money.

I had nothing but a good-luck charm.
I had supernatural power.

I did not want to play the organ—
I had no wish to marry. I wanted to
dance with the young men in town—
I wanted to dance till they hunted me down.

The Idiots and the Beersoakers

They are in charge of the revels at
Five Miles from Anywhere—No hurry,
Our room had a headless skeleton in the
cupboard—it terrified Matthew so much
he could hardly sleep.

Oh Matthew, Matthew! God will turn your
body to stone before the night is over,
I have seen you playing a game of chance,
talking strangely to your silent partner,
walking arm in arm with your strange partner.

Grey Ladies and Brown Ladies

I am disfigured by wounds,
Annie Walker. Mutilated,
Margaret Evans.

Ladies of shade, of shadow and
darkness; grey ladies and brown ladies
attend me.

I go into witch-country with a
dowry of wild cattle. No neck,

tiny legs and tongueless in a wet
winter—who would marry it?

I gave Godrich fifteen children—
still he beheaded me for adultery.

Like War, Like Marriage

Isobel, Isobel
let in no lovers.
Are you still faithful on your
death bed? Are you letting it happen?

Isobel, death is sly.
You should not wear white,
you should not paint your face or
show a leg to the male nurses.

Death wants to share everything.
He wants to get under the covers

he wants to get on

he's panting to get on.

A Man to Marry, a Man to Bury
1979

I. Flying the Flag of Ourselves

Crossing to Brentwood on the Mill Bay Ferry—November 4, 1975

Now, for the moment, everything is promised.
It is a calm bright day.
Not even any mist over the trees,
nor ice in the slippery roots.
No sense of urgency.

We are crossing the water.
I hold your hand needing
only that. The bare sea is simple enough
and the clean sky that no longer seems
lonely. Birds circle the boat
full of their good messages.

Last night snow fell on the
mountains. I woke up
shivering and afraid.
I needed to know everything about you.
Suddenly I needed to know
more than what there was.

Today, for the moment, everything is forgotten.
I hold your warm hand as if it were something
I had just found wanting to be held and
you smile back. Later when we talk
ours will be other voices.
Now, crossing the water,
I am certain there is only us.

You Are on a Train

You are on a train coming down
from the mountains, coming closer and
closer; you have been travelling for a
long time.

Nobody is expecting you.
Your cheek against the glass is cold,
is white. A bird lifts up from a winter
tree, flies toward you out of the distance
as your train begins its slow descent into
poisoned farmland.

You are dreaming, you dream you are
sleeping. Where you are coming from is
cold. You do not remember the name of that
country.

I am not expecting you.
I have made up your bed and closed the curtains.
I have hung your picture back in its place,
put on an old dress, arranged my face.
I have filled my body with your silence; still
I am not expecting you.

You are on a train
you are glad to be travelling
happy to be going somewhere finally,
finally arriving.

You have no memory of the past.
You have no expectations.
You are alone on a train coming down
from the mountains, coming closer and
closer, flying toward me out of the distance.

Fishing on a Snowy Evening

How close you come
to being alone.
How close you come
to needing no one.

River is silent, silver
over stone. You are a link
between air and water.

You are alive.
You cast your line out
into the cool shallows;
river rises into shadow
secret and heavy.

A fish jumps.
River ripples and bends—
how close you come
to your own reflection.
Your body surfaces and breaks—
how close you come
to perfection.

Snow falls from the cold
sky, snow covers your closed
eyes. It drifts into your
deep tracks, over the way you
came, over the way back.

How close you come
to innocence at this moment,
how close you come to emptiness.

Snow falls down
out of the cold sky.
It fills your narrowing hours.

Growth of the Soil

You were planting a garden.
The earth was too wet, too
rich, you said

and took a photograph of me
instead

digging last year's borders.

The moon was coming over my
right shoulder as if you had
planted her there. That explained
my working long into the late evening.

Don't Die on the Highway

speeding toward light, the night
behind you, the night

inside your rearview mirror
igniting the whole sky.

Your eyes are ice,
broken glass on the road at night

you are driving toward the moon,
driving alive out of the night sky.

It is my heart that beats in the
moon's breast, my eyes that mirror the
moon's reflection.

I do not want to share her with
anyone. Remember, it is my moon,
my moon.

What Do You Do When the Moon Is Blue

and you're drifting toward
Vermilion, Saskatoon.
I'm at the end of the line and
you're just passing through.

It's a wide wide country
wild and wide
and I'm not familiar
with where you've been.
You are always driving
and never arriving

I'm watching the tide roll in.

Where do you go
when the moon is blue
it hardly ever happens

when it happens, it's real.

It's hard to understand,
difficult to feel. Like the
sun and the moon sharing the
same sky, you see

nothing lasts

nothing lives for long

nothing burns forever
in that sky.

Flying the Flag of Ourselves

because we have no country,
no place to return to other than
our own bodies

because we are alone
and have reached this place
together

because there is no one to
pray for us,
no one to worship.

It is the flag of innocence,
of joy and celebration.
When we look into each other's eyes
it is reflected there—
we see it is the flag of loneliness.

It is a beautiful flag,
it fills up the whole sky.

It is the flag we fly
because we are alive

the flag of our union
you, love, and I.

The God of Love

On our first night together
there were sirens
and a new moon

and no doubt there were
different people

turning to one another
in different parts of the city.

It didn't matter;
that's why we had each other.

It was more than just enough
but nevertheless something troubled me.
I moved from our bed to the window
where it was bright. The whole world
around me seemed to be on fire.

The air was black
and breathing became difficult.
I knew I had been mistaken:
I saw that fire was much more than
sudden brightness.

Nothing could have been colder,
I had not dreamed of anything so
dark. The people ran about
crying out to the god who created them.
*The sight of their vulnerable bodies made me
feel humble.*

That was when I drew back to touch you,
knowing we could never wake
before the flames reached us.

Right Through the Heart

and out the other side,
pumping like a bitch in heat,
beast with two backs, the
left and right ventricles.

It has to be love
when it goes straight through;

no bone can stop it,
no barb impede its journey.

When it happens you have to bleed,
you want to kiss and hold on

despite all the messy blood
you want to embrace it.

You want it to last forever,
you want to own it.
You want to take love's tiny life
in your hands

and crush it to death before it dies.

Without Title

I wanted to write
a kind of love poem

simply to say this:

that nothing is simple,
not even holding you now

lying together, lost on the
same bed,

the whole world inside us
an unborn child

that has no father
or mother.

When You Lie Down, Lie With Me

This is war.
This is real.
This is living together.
This is loving one man and
leaving another.

This is trying to keep warm.
This is trying to stay alive.
This is trying to remember
how you turned in the bed

how you looked at me then

and turned again.

It Is the Night

I wake up blind.
I wake up with my heart beating.
I wake up looking for something familiar.
I wake up bleeding.

I wake up wishing I could
sleep forever.
I wake up beside a man who smiles and says
Good Morning.
I wake up deaf.
I wake up full of regret.
I wake up looking for someone to blame
for the fact that my life is
commonplace and solitary.

I wake up wanting to die.
I wake up waiting.

When it is time to dream
I wake up. It is the night,
the real night.

Eddy

I have left you again.
Tonight you lie in a room with no
windows.
I am walking down Main Street
in a tight black dress,
walking away laughing;
there is something about my leaving that is
final.

It wasn't the loneliness,
it wasn't the cruelty,
it wasn't your heavy body even
that kept us warm and wanting one another.

Finally I am alone.
There must be a thousand men like you.
There must be someone like you somewhere.
In the whole world somehow there must be at least
a stranger.

I have left you again.
I have a picture of us in my pocket.
I stole it while you were sleeping.
We are walking down Main Street together,
walking along laughing.

In the photograph you are younger.
There is something about you that is innocent.
You hold on to me as if you have nothing more
to live for.
There is something about my leaving that is
beautiful, beautiful.

Returning to the Town Where We Used to Live

I found this photograph.

A woman is reaching toward you.
Your hands seem to meet
where now my own fall uselessly.
Even the air around me is cruel,
and your creaturely eyes
full of a new hunger.

I seem to have been travelling
all my life. Your last letter written
ages ago says nothing has ended.

Returning to the town where
we used to live
I found this photograph.

A woman is leaning toward you.
Your eyes seem to meet where now
I feel only a stranger.
I had wanted to be so much.
I seem to have been travelling forever.

Just yesterday I flew
over the country where you live,
knowing I would never find you,
knowing I never did.

I saw the new moon holding
the old moon in her arms

I wanted to be held
and to hold you like this.

II. The Embalmer's Art

Between Friends

This is the field where he died all right.
Caught his neck up in baling wire.
Head popped clean as a bull's pizzle
with as much again inside.
We didn't do much planting that year.
It pays to give the ground a rest.

This is the spot all right.
His son went the same way
only he did it with dynamite.
You might say there was a
family tradition. He would have been
seventeen last month.

The old woman got kind of crazy
after that and kept saying there was this
frog from her stomach. She chopped up
her sister's kid and cooked it.
Last I heard she'd taken her own life.

Between you and me, it isn't much worth
talking about. It was common enough
in those days, anyhow.
Death and that.

Time Out

It's come back.
I mean that miscarried
spidery growth I keep

tucked up in my head.
Neatly sealed off it is,
usually. Crusty as old
cow-pats only sometimes
when I'm lonely it starts to hurt.

Of course it hurts.
It always does at first.
You learn to enjoy every bit of it.
It's like having a secret you
have to share with everyone.

All exterminators have secrets.

Just think of those leper girls
and the plague burial pits.
Just think of the barbecue and the
ritual stink.

There's no easy coupling in a
narrow grave; you'd want a saint
like me around with death warrants and
handkerchiefs.

I carry it all
right here in my head. Nobody
is forgotten. I am history's
executioner.

That's what this growth thing
is all about—I give suicide
the trophy. Watch out for that
forked stick, it could be
crippling. You're bound to be hearing
more about this.

J Did Jt to Attract Women

he said; there was no question
of an appeal. He had dressed them up
carefully and tried to conceal the blood.
After his initial disgust over their
badly decomposing bodies he took turns
telling them stories at night.

He had tried to make them eat but their
smell was sickening. They wouldn't cooperate,
they made him feel trapped. Their constant
quarrelling drove him to distraction. This was how
he came finally with their crushed heads to the
police station—calling God as his witness—
a good family man.

Killing Time

Someone is dead.
Someone is dead and
no one is grieving.

We all sang songs instead
and smiled on like undertakers.
We called each other on the
telephone, speaking just out of
earshot.

Someone suggested we get rid
of the body so we loaded it
into a taxi. It was
Saturday night and
raining like romance
so someone suggested we
cancel our other arrangements.

Being young and easy and knowing
nothing better

we chained the piano player
to a rousing piece, and watched.

Outside all the old girls laughed
out of long-established habit,
all tits and ass with heads like
lumpen vegetables. They were
loving us stiff when the
stink of that corpse caught up.

All those offertory bags
snapped shut.
All those tantalizing sighs
disintegrated.

Someone said
something is dead.
We just looked at each other.

Someone suggested we all go home
in the same taxi, being young and late and
having no alternative.

We took the familiar route,
reticent as ever,
swerving only once to avoid
some undeserving animal.

Old Sheep on the Road Near Cleggan, the West of Ireland

In Connemara
there is one wanting to die.

He beats his head on a rock
and the rock breaks.

He lies down alone
in the calm road.
He waits and waits.

The right birds
do not come for his eyes;
I do not stop to help, either.

We look the way the good Sisters
look, to say "Where does it pain?"
and close the lights.

There is one wanting to do much more than live.

Even the butchers evade him.

Failing to Remain

> *Death, the driver, abandoned his*
> *motorcycle and fled on foot.*
> *—News of the World*

We all do the wrong thing sometimes;
maybe had a weak moment or a pressing engagement.
They made him sound like a criminal when the fact is
many of us would do the same in his position.

They sniffed him out eventually, he'd barely left
the scene of the accident. Why he didn't get clean away
I'll never know—he must have been curious.

He wouldn't make a statement—his guilt was
indisputable. He didn't cooperate with the press either
but why should he they only wanted a good story.

I was called as a witness but chose to maintain silence.
I was a passenger at the time—I had only gone along
for the ride.

Tom Navy

Bill he goes staggerin back, eh
to get Gloria. A whole bunch of us
had been drinkin up at the pub—
Tom he was the only Indian who could walk
and he was walkin on crutches.

That night it was so cold your ass froze.
Twenty-seven of us sleepin in two rooms—
Charlie he goes fallin through the floor
shit man he was pissed faceless with
Tom Navy smokin up down below
drinkin rum and Drano, man
a crazy bastard.

Charlie—that's Bill's brother—
he dies, eh—chokin.
Billy he goes for Gloria but she
won't come.
She's scared shitless of Tom.
Gloria, that's Charlie and them's old lady.

Tom Navy takes his knife, eh
and starts hackin. Jeez it was cold
but Tom he didn't seem to feel nothin.

He starts carvin some new legs,
that's what he says he's carvin.
Gloria seen him shoot the last pair off
himself—he just about died laughin.

Man, I gotta do somethin about old Charlie.
Man, I gotta *do* somethin.

Non-Status Indians' Bingo Song

I've got a picture of you daddy
in the back of my head
you're lucky you are still alive
and I am dead.

It's Saturday night
and I'm looking for fun
looking for an Indian
a good-looking one.

It won't be Johnny Yes
and it won't be Johnny No
I'm looking for the man named
Johnny Bingo.

It's a dangerous night
in a small-town bar
but I'm betting on the devil
in the beat-up car.

Johnny's riding shotgun
and I'm lying low
Johnny takes his time
he's got no place left to go.

I did it because I loved him
I did it because I'm White
I did it for Johnny Bingo
I'll do it again tonight.

I've got a picture of you daddy
in the back of my head
you're lucky you are still alive
you're lucky I am dead.

The British Migraine Association Poetry Competition

Winning poems will be published
in the anthology.
The title of the anthology will be
NIGHT RIDE TO SUNRISE,
and this will also be the
theme of the competition.
The title is taken from the
tone poem of Sibelius
in which the music depicts a
horseman riding through the night.
After a long, solitary and
exhausting ride through darkness,
the sun finally breaks through.
All poems submitted should
relate to the theme,
however loosely.
The theme is symbolic
and should not be treated
literally.
No poem should be given the
same title as the theme.
We wish all entrants to
bear in mind that everyone,
of all ages and nationalities,
suffers conflicts either personal
or of world-shattering proportions;
trivial or insignificant,
or major and devastating.
We all experience problems,
disabilities, depressions and
struggle,
then through resolution,
determination and endurance
often overcome them,

or at least live with them.
Sometimes we fail.
The poems submitted need not have
a positive conclusion,
but they must have
some bearing on the theme,
however remote.
They may deal with only one
aspect of the theme
symbolized by either the
"night ride" or the
"sunrise".
They may relate to nature
or the universe; may be
symbolic or abstract.
They may offer hope or despair,
humour or tragedy;
they may be serious or
merely frivolous. Indeed,
the problems may not be
human at all.

Found on the
entry form

Salad Days

This poet describes carbon paper, how it lies flat
and impressionable between two sheets of white.
He cannot begin to digest such feelings of inferiority.
The audience is being prepared.

A tree is about to fall on the crowd as
this one executes his poem. It is not supposed to be
comedy when the chain saw fells the poet by mistake.
The audience is full of anticipation;
hard hats are being distributed under the exit sign.

This poet displays a growing tolerance toward
frivolity. She crouches behind the microphone
crunching a wild turnip.
The audience is unusually sober.

This poet makes homemade brew in his bath.
He is disrespectful of his wife.
He wears dark glasses and a string of medals.
He has never been to war in his life.
"More," they cry, "more!"

This poet is in pain. She is professional in her
romanticism. She bares her chest and lops off her
breasts. The knife goes on display at the university.
The audience is satisfied.

Then there is the usual round of applause.
The poets bow to one another, exchange hands and
stagger out. Back home in the bar they liquidate their
     profits.
The audience remains fixed, fresh for another season.

"Recognition Not Enough"

Today there is
damage being done.
Damage unrewarded in the
history books of the law.

Damage being done to the
children, waking in the
too-bright sun.
Damage being done to the
eloquent, the lascivious.

Damage is being done to the
ordinary, to the invalids
in their frail carriages.

Damage is being done to the
whole world, to all the
nodding, careering people.
They are bandaging one another,
bandaging the damage.

Even the artists with their
crude tools, or doctors
with their cool instruments—
even the undertakers,
they cannot stop the damage.

I flutter my tiny hands,
useless, useless.
I undo my dress,
it is useless, useless.
I see weapons twitching in
grisly fingers.
It is useless, useless.
I smell blood and guts and begin
to feel generous.

Damage is being done to everyone.
It keeps us nasty.

The Embalmer's Art

is poetry. Of a kind, mind you,
and not to suit everybody's taste.

But this is not a poem for just
anybody. No, in fact, it is meant
for my family.

It is a poem to strangers, then,
on the occasion of Christmas. We sit
sipping smart cocktails, funereal almost

in our elaborate decoration. Around us the room
is dangerously lit.

Every year it is the same ritual—
it sounds quite normal I know and I
suppose it is. *Smile, smile.* I unwrap
each gift with the same cautious enthusiasm
in which it was no doubt chosen.
My young brothers twitch and their
tinselly wives twitter. My mother laughs too
in spite of my own happiness.
Even my father the undertaker is smiling to himself
as he opens another box and quietly closes it again.

Due Process
after an article by Ben Metcalfe

So there was this
small celebration in the
prison kitchen afterward,
with doughnuts and
well-laced coffee and
idle talk of the last
double-noose ceremony.

One of the boys took seventeen minutes
to die. The other,
twenty-three. They fell together
without a sound
though you could see from their eyes
they had been weeping recently.

They say a good hangman
is hard to find;
a good man is even harder.

Hobbled out, prayed over
trussed bagged noosed and dropped

strangulation completes the process
sooner or later.

III. The Angel-Maker

Witchfinder General

Small comfort is this
hell-hound at my heels,
sniffing out the slightest whiff
of heresy. He has grown old and
familiar; demon-dog at the
supernumerary nipple.

Lonely old crones, they suck me
up. I should be lonelier riding the
long roads, waking and walking,
devising new ways of obtaining
confessions.

The Widow Weed with her
witch-mark; I found her.
Isobel Long and Rebecca Swan,
I found them. I accused them of
cursing, of driving pigs mad and
sailing through a sieve.

No torture was brutal enough,
they felt no pain.
No death was final enough,
they were incapable of bleeding.

Many of them burned
proclaiming their innocence;
I had to stake them to the earth
to prevent them from rising.

No grave was secure from those
false gods they worshipped;
my own God ordered me to find witches,
to suffer them not and murder without mercy.

The Angel-Maker

> Angel-makers. That's what they
> used to call abortionists.
> —Margaret Laurence, *A Jest of God*

I am old, my horoscope has run out.
My headdress terrifies you, I know,
but let me assure you one mask only conceals another.

You knew this already. Try to be patient.
I have no religion really, just a scalp lock for
good luck and a handful of beads.
They come to me needing, they come on their knees.
They come with devotion, they come for me.

All the animals in the forest, all the birds are
weeping. I alone can hear them—I have not been spared
those powers. Yet look—you cry too. Read a book,
get some work to do.

I will put on more rags, I will paint my face
for you. Orange, grey, royal blue. One bulging,
black false eye. I will smile on the world that waves,
a brittle flower on a blind stalk.

Look up at the stars, those elements of
augery. This child would be born wanting—

sweet shock for his indigent father. See, I have
three fingers and each one honed to a murderous art.
Relax, please, this is no place for moral prudery.

A weak stomach, perhaps?
Or blood is not a strong point in your personal
constitution? It is the death of yourself you must
fathom, not the depth. Do not give in to guilt, try.
Oh this self-effacing ceremony!

That painting there—it is my most memorable
possession. A gift for pathos, you might say,
my licence to practise. See, the woman visits the
grave of her child by moonlight. The diffused light
helps to set it off, don't you think—obscures the
sentiment.

So move from the bed. I must know your face.
Come let us not be ungracious to that audience which has
long entertained me. By that I mean you are one of
many. You insist on knowing? *As many as can dance on the
point of a needle.* Frivolous, you must think me, but
it was your choice. No doubt this is what *she* is
thinking—that woman in the picture.

I should be more generous. Take my hand—
yes it is fragile and unshakable, not what you expected.
Look in the mirror; everything is waving. *Goodbye, goodbye.*
Every habit, every gift, every hesitant drift.
Look up at the sky. Somebody is waiting.

Woodcutter, River-God and J

When I first came to the river
I was afraid to cross. It was a
river of ice in a season of ice
and my cold cries echoed like the
tolling of spectral bells.

A woodcutter lived in the woods
beyond the river—I could hear
his ghostly song. He was carving
a woman, an offering to the river-
god. She was an angel of mystery,
all witchery.

It was the winter solstice, the
sacrifice. I filled up my shoes
with ice. I filled up my warm body
with ice. Even the black dogs of
Odin with their jaws dripping fire,
even the oyster-fattened cats with
their claws gripping—and my gripped
heart; everything was frozen.

The old man came down to the river,
the woodcutter. His eye was like
snakebite, my skin milkwhite. He
took my hand, shivering as it was,
and the river cracked. There were
white bears under the ice who woke
and he spoke to them.

They were curious. They rose like
apparitions from their coffins lined
with snow. They nodded their white
heads like white weathervanes though
there was no wind.

They were messengers from the dead—
the old man led me out across the ice.
On the far shore waited the river-god;
he was expecting someone. I told him
I had no reason to go on, no reason
to turn back either.

The ice was melting—the whole world
thawing and shifting. Even my body

warmed, my witch-heart warmed to his
cool offering. The waters were rising
but we sat casting pebbles like bored
anglers.

More mysterious than angels, river-god,
woodcutter and I sat watching the white
bears. They were fleeing to higher
ground, wading inland as the world
ended. Three survivors with no future
we sat uncaring as the world ended—

as if there were anywhere we could go.

Picking Cloudberries by Moonlight

under the powdery stars
and trudging home later
over frozen ground with
first light breaking

everything was easy.

Ice formed in our footsteps
as if where we were coming from
was a thousand years ago.
Ice grew on my fingers around the glass,
on the berries inside like
blood clots barely pulsing.

With you wearing the old green
jacket that still holds your shape
even now long after you have
abandoned it; with you holding
your new knife and that weapon
I had suddenly grown curious of

everything seemed easy.

Often I have tried to remember
why you stopped, with me shivering at the
road's edge anxious to go on. So often
I have wanted to remember the way we took,
as if what we had been hoping to find
had little to do with the search.

Then the shining lake,
the insomniac moon.
Birds rose up out of the ice
(it seemed to take place over centuries);
frightened by our own awkwardness
you reached to draw me back.

Crouched down under a dead tree
for shelter we watched them, all
colours and music. It was ghostly;
you said *wait for me.* I never knew choice
until that moment.

Clutching my cold jar of
berries as if it were fire to
comfort us or light to lead you
from whatever I felt unsure of

I walked away.

Yet waking alone in a strange world
even later, still hearing you say *wait*
but not having had the courage,
everything is forgiven.

I do not remember the gun going off.
I have tried to forget this much.

Drinking Raw Vodka on the Railway Tracks

with Bucky McGuire and
Gabrielle on some kind of a
bad trip

after a sober breakfast
and me deciding best not to
interfere anyway

leaving them alone after a
long mile of old conversation,
Gabrielle wanting to
hold my arm

and me, having known her once,
having no last wish to intrude.

At Grizzly's Clump I heard
wild cattle pawing and heaving like
old whores

I heard Gabrielle laugh.

Turning my back on all thoughts of
going on, trying to drink my own life
out of my mind

I heard her shout.

*It sounded like laughter, or weeping—
panic maybe. I never cared until
afterward.*

Finding them wasn't easy
days later

the whole town, the bloodhound,
sniffing across the snow

bringing them home was no easier,
later on her cheap scent
unstiffening with her wounds.

And Bucky McGuire, the old boot,
refusing to thaw.

We buried them in the same box
in that rigid graveyard growing
colder and more unfeeling

with me thinking suddenly
about the animal
everyone believed in going after—

the gravediggers impatient to be gone

the last train echoing, echoing.

Carnival

I only remember the rats,
he said. Nothing else, no,
not even the tired grey women
selling tickets to the
tunnel of love.

Not the bodies of the young girls
blooming like caught sails
under the sky, or monks
in their sensuous robes, fingering
their delicate lutes.

Not even the balloon man with his
spotted dog, nor the drinking

jester, nor the faith healer
with a little bowl in his hands.

I remember counting the rats.
One night there were eight of them
sharing the shabby bedsit.

They became an obsession.
In the morning when you woke
to face a soft underbelly it was
delectable nostalgia. Weapons
were futile; you pitted yourself
against their skills.

You were a fellow sufferer.
You found your identity in
wiping them away. For days at a time
you had nothing else to eat.
But even rats cannot stop
dullness creeping in.

I started dreaming of women.
Their split sex seemed an enigma,
monstrous. I had no wish for such
meaningless opulence.

My foraging became inhuman.
I gorged myself nightly beneath
beer cellars and dancehalls.
I saw how dangerous my own waste
had become, and social barriers
nonexistent.

I only remember the rats.
It was their ruthlessness I admired,
their lack of religion. I took hold of them
in my hands, squeezing life out of them
as gently as you would shake laughter out of
children.

Perhaps *they* were laughing at the
indignities I made them suffer. In the end
their pain was more welcome than a friend.

But their suffering was far more
permanent than my own: when one died
there was always a replacement.

I remember the rats,
he said. Nothing else, no,
only the rats.
Not the tired grey women
selling tickets to the
tunnel of love, not even
the bodies of the young girls.

Coming of Age

The pit at midnight
crusty with snow
like day-old bread pudding

and Giffey the outlaw
giving a sermon about sin

right down there
in a preacher's black gown

only his cock and his
cloven hoof peeping out a little.

The chalk pit where
Giffey would show us his stump.
We used to line up for him,
undaunted by his obscene gestures.

And show him *our* proud bodies.

All nine of us, nubile and
cheeky, dancing just out of his
reach

and old Giffey getting all creamy
and churned up
with each of us worrying and wriggling
like that.

We were so quick
we teased him until he came,
blasting off into the moonlight
for all the world to watch.

Then he would cry
and we thought he was crazy,
not daring to come close or
touch, not near enough for
comfort.

We were the peaty source of his
darkness, with our lies and our smiles
and stories about our lives.
For there were no blessings in our cold
eyes, only cruelty, and more of that for
our youth.

At night I would dream of
giving myself to him,
being drilled into the dirt,
cursing and carrying on like
old Giffey himself when his
wormy thing wouldn't get hard.

I saw myself kneeling below him,
opening myself before him,
lying open beneath him

tightening and tempting

until one night he never
came anymore.

We were haunted and stripped
naked at last, eager for
whatever unpleasantness he would
permit

anxious for all his ungainliness:

he never came.

Colder than ever in that chalk
pit tracing circles with our toes

we crept home finally to our
clean beds, long past the usual
hour, completed and alone.

A Curious Centurion

I met him on a mountain
black cowl covering his head
a sniper in the heather he led
me down into the stony pasture

cushioned my heart on a fleshy pillow,
fed me spiced milk on a ruined altar.

He lived on the mountain, he said,
lured holy men and saints to go that way
on pilgrimage. I was lucky to get off
with my life; being a child saved me.

His legions were deserting, delivered
out of the melancholy of armour.

From my damp bed I heard the tramp of the
corpse carriers; bog ghosts croaking like
gods unworshipped.

I prayed for him, a devil's dark prayer—
haunted over the bare slopes, hunted
through a dry season. I had a tin drum
and a toy gun, a gambler's wild hand and
a warrior's reason.

War was all around; the deceitful moon
rose with undefeatable custom. She shone
with more cunning than the fusty prophets
of my cursed village. There was always a
war going on. My father had his own gun,
and it was real.

I remember the humming of wild bees,
an old sheep with no eyes, those
far-seeing ravens. I climbed to that
church where the marble deity lay fallen,
a shrine desecrated and unholy.

I remember the shadow on the cross
carried by warm winds over the warm grass

and the song of the soldiers going home
at last

whitehorn in their helmets,
flags of surrender.

The Judas Goat

It was a bad sign I was born under,
half animal, half a cruel joke of nature.
The antlered ghosts of my ancestors were
vanishing; I envied them their shifty universe.

Fate made me plain and bitter,
my shape more symbol than pathfinder or
builder. I wandered from the herd to
escape humiliation—found more misery there
than mystery.

Where I grazed along the wayside
nothing would grow; when I lay down in the
garbage I gave no thought to the flowers.
Skirting the world's edge I thrived on spoils,
glutted my maw, grew reconciled to hunger.

Returning to the flock restored my
dignity. The fat ewes gathered to greet me;
I spoke to them in their own language.
Where I led them to drink there was a warm trough and
plenty to eat. There was a dry place to
lie down; my ease did not betray cowardice.

Lord of everything pleasurable and defenceless,
I woke to their calling resurrected and holy.
There was no need for treachery in their
measure of life; too simple by origin they
followed me to the slaughterhouse.

My power was inimitable and blinding.
When they smelled their own blood they were
no longer afraid. They stumbled and fell
as if my will had supported them. I watched them
weakening, unashamed.

Even their whimpering made me feel ruthless,
the greatness of conquest far greater than
self-sacrifice. But when they lifted their
gentle heads to remind me all would be forgiven,
I turned and looked away.

There on the solitary block I sprawled
rootless and agonizing, Lord God of lolling tongues,
deliverer of carnage.

I prayed I had not become human.

IV. Salmonberry Road

To Clo-oose and Whyack,
west coast of Vancouver Island, June 1977

1. Doubt Being the Measure of Worth

Part of every journey is
not wanting to go on

not wanting to get there,
to take risks   and so on

Marilyn had a moment of doubt
in Nitinat Camp   Wednesday morning
after a long drive in   through
                          Lake Cowichan and
Caycuse

      we were going to   Clo-oose
we'd planned it for some time
having come this far

      Michael and I were determined to
keep moving.

We rented a boat from Mike Thompson
he said he would bring us up the
lake after lunch

the lake being a bit
choppy

dangerous in fact

Marilyn said it was
famous for being dangerous and
untied her hiking boots
just in case.

In the boat I felt the fine spray
over my neck and face
I admit I had a moment
of doubt myself
wondering
if the boat was safe.

But out there on the lake I was
happier than I'd ever been before
far away from confusion
the kind of happiness
I could trust
the kind of happiness
that is not possible.

Nothing existed beyond that moment
beyond the far edges of the lake
the three of us
smiling
the three of us together for the
first time in the boat built by Mike Thompson's
late father.

Oh my ancestors if you could see me now
floating and drifting
alive and dreaming
if you could wake up out of your long sleep
long enough to breathe again this

> *breathing earth*

these living rocks   this tide
this   lichen-carrying wind

I would be happy to welcome you
you would be welcome to share my happiness.

When I am old I swear I shall remember this day.
When I am too old to go anywhere I shall
remember sharing an orange with Mike Thompson in
Brown's Cove after we safely landed.

2. What We Found on the First Day

Marilyn found an eagle's feather
somebody had made into a pen

a good omen

it didn't surprise any of us.

Michael found a salmon
it was hardly alive but
swimming   poor thing
they both   killed it

Michael and Marilyn

I guess they did the
right thing
still I felt sorry for it

and didn't eat any myself.

Marilyn also found an
archaeopteryx
it had been dead for some time

but she resurrected it

a good emblem.

Michael found
wood and water

that was useful

I found a human skull on a
stick

it hardly surprised anyone.

3. The First Night

a small bird with fur
came to eat out of my hands

a small bird without wings
or feathers.

Spirit of the sea mist
his bones were trembling

in the moonlight we made a nest
out of small sea flowers.

4. It Is Simple, Here

lying around the fire all
afternoon in the hot, hot
sun watching a few eagles
in the trees

it is simple, here

we take turns making tea.

When all the biscuits
have been eaten

we make do.

5. Sooner or Later

you'll have to face the eagles,
Michael said

they are part of the scenery here
you can't just ignore them.

We had been talking about death
up until that point

and the eagles were circling us.

Suddenly one of them
dropped out of the sky

Michael I cried

I'm alive! I'm alive!

6. Isabella Valancy Crawford

your name goes over and over again
in my head as I'm walking down this
trail

walking down the Salmonberry Road
to Whyack.

It could be because Marilyn was
talking about you earlier

it could be because I'm so tired
of walking.

All I know is
your name keeps me going
like a charm I keep saying it
over and over

Isabella Valancy Crawford
Isabella Valancy Crawford.

When we stop to rest your name
keeps me going

(I had a brief moment of anger
when the trail became impassable.)

7. Whyack, Village of Witchcraft

Marilyn saw them first,
weird women by the graveyard
opening the guestbook.

She told them
we weren't visitors,
we were planning to leave
immediately.

The old houses facing the sea
are forgotten;
in every window a widow,
in every grave a reason.

8. Old House at Clo-oose

Downstairs it's like every
other house in the neighbourhood,
rusty bedsprings and old mattresses
with no sleep left in them
and Michael calls me to come
upstairs—he has a better view
of the village.

I find dolls, badly mutilated.
I want to mend them and mend them.
I want to take them away with me.
I want to defend them.

Oh Michael Michael
I saw your ghost last night in a
dream

gentle and dreaming, you needed
mending too.

I wanted to touch you, but only
for a moment.
The knife in my hands will not pause
for your love, nor your life, nor any cause.

9. Two Letters Found in the House

December 11, 1953

Dear Jane to just tell you
to come down on the returns boat
and go to mrs andrew james
and I'll pick you up there
take all children with you

302

I am sending $10.00
ten dollars
for your fare

If you have little take a
state room

I am giving you a chance
to pull your teeth

Henry Tate that canoe in the
shed belongs to Jerry Sthels

he paid for it already

June 15, 1965

Hi there Jo-Ann
i just thought i'd write you a
letter see or ask how you are.
How are you? hope o.k.
For me i got a head-ache
a ear trouble toe trouble oh well!
Just kidding. What are you doing?
Swimming, trouting, fishing,
kissing, oh jeez.
Me i'm just writing letters this
morning and i gotta to go out and
mail them to-day.

All the men are gone. They went
yester-day, icing.
There's just me and Mae left.

How is your Mom and sister Phyllis
tell them i said hello.

Boy there's nothing to do
i got up with my house-work.

Last night i watched T.V.
it was real good.
Just me sat up and watched
it was a murder story.

Well in the evening i'll be going
evening fishing in Richard's putter
he said i could so i guess i will.
Boy it sure dead since you have gone.
I sure miss you.
Oh yeah Dick's going with Joe Garcia
icing so i guess he's left yester-day.
He sure looks blue.
When you guys getting married?
Soon. I'll throw 5lbs. of rice
over you o.k.

Well friend i must close for now.
Write soon.
Excuse my writing i'm in a rush and
gotta to go out and mail these
letters.
Bye from a friend.

Marie Nookemus

10. Letter to Marilyn Gone to Scotland— July 5, 1977

Anyway you've gone now
and after you left i said
goodbye to the dog for you
because you asked me to

and then there was your
tea cup to rinse out and

put away and the smell of
your lingering perfume
lingering just like it does
in certain kinds of
sentimental music

anyway it's gone now
and i have just written
these poems from Clo-oose

("we were there once,
we knew each other")

Michael he's gone too
and i gotta to go into town
and guess what (oh jeez)
i got this real bad pain in my
heart again

just like last winter

anyway it's gone now
and i thought i would write
friend to say i sure
miss you but

i'm not going to be lonely
i'm not going to be lonely
i'm not going to be lonely

V. Even in the Ordered World

"Dig, He Said, Dig"

Today I brought home
an ankle bone.

I found it when I was
digging, digging, digging.

Today I brought home
a knife made of stone.
I found it when I was
digging, digging, digging.

The knife was not clean,
nor the bone,
nor were my hands afterward.

I buried you too soon,
though not deep enough.
I am still digging, digging.

"What the Small Day Cannot Hold"
for Brian Patten

All night I lay awake
thinking it was you.
All night I lay thinking
maybe it was.

All night I hung like a
child's moon above the trees,
swinging above the clouds, even,
and higher than that, the sun.
All night I lay thinking
about everyone I had ever loved.
I wanted to give their love back.

I wanted to give back the moon
and the clouds as well.
I wanted to give back the sun
and everything that glittered.

All night I lay dreaming
of how it had to be done.
All night I lay thinking
maybe it was.

Maybe it was your shadow
crossing the child's grave.
Maybe it was you
who left such little flowers.

Wedding Song

She signs away the moon.
She signs away the wind and the stars.

She signs away cities,
she signs away men and women.

She builds a life out of the
ashes of children.
she signs away the fire.

The flowers go on opening.

She puts her signature to the
slippery black rocks,
to the winter earth,
to wild sage and peppermint.
She signs away darkness,
she signs away the sun.

The flowers go on opening.

By the ocean she sees
a graveyard filling up.
She puts her signature to the
unmarked graves,

to the ringing chapel,
the dead bell.

She signs away the earth,
she signs away water.

The flowers go on opening.

The beautiful flowers.

North Beach Birth
for Jennie and Ghin

The first month is over.
A spirit smiles in the
woman's bed—his two teeth
like a little walrus!
Crow on Tow Hill
flies up laughing—
joins your small hands to mine,
your dark eyes to mine.

The second month is over.
A seed wakes from sleep in the
woman's house—the man is
hauling up halibut.
Whale at Nai-Tas-Cudley
dives down flashing—
joins your soft breasts to mine,
your smooth lips to mine.

The third month is over.
Blood gathers, drop by drop—
the kayak-man's oars are red with blood.
Otter off Rose Spit
swims out crying—

joins your sad ghost to mine,
your sorrow to mine.

The fourth month is over.
Bones dance in the woods—
the white-bone edges are red with blood.
Eagle at the Oeanda
soars up singing—
joins your quiet song to mine,
your silence to mine.

The fifth month is over.
A heart beats in the night—
Spirit, Spirit, Spirit!
Deer at Yagan Village
lies down sleeping—
joins your long journey to mine,
your dreams to mine.

The sixth month is over.
A shape shifts in the dank roots,
trembles into life.
Bear at Gul-Ah-Yonun
wakes up hungry—
joins your warm things to mine,
your round belly to mine.

The seventh month is over.
A name is found—for the rain,
for the wind, for the earth.
Frog at Cleet-Ots-Unas
leaps up dancing—
joins your black shadow to mine,
your magic to mine.

The eighth month is over.
A voice fills up the whole sky—
Ayi! Yai! Ya!
Octopus at Hoyagundla

sinks down smiling—
joins your gentleness to mine,
your secret to mine.

The ninth month is over.
A child is born:
listen, listen, listen!
Raven at Kliki Damen
flaps off croaking—
joins your own life to mine,
your whole life to mine.

Deadfall

Always with the trap in mind
he enters her body.
It is not warm, but icy,
and even though he comes honestly
by his own choice,
she will not hold him.

Others have offered this heat,
tottered back against
ice ages gently receding.
She lies as the cold allows,
deceives no one.

Always with the noose in his mind
he comes slowly, knowing the
baited hook, the slow poison.
Her body is a crushed thing
on the clean white earth.
There is nothing to say
how broken, how untouched.

Break-Up
for David Arnason

All your life he has
lived in you, the
ice fish. He has fed on
edges, on extremities.
All your life you have been an
ice fisherman. Frozen and
hungry you are finally breaking.

You count the lonely minutes.
You count the hours.
Your heart beats against the breaking,
rages against the beating.

Your gentle hands are nets,
are knives. Your eyes remember a time
before the ice shifted.

Break a hole in the ice,
let the fish breathe.
Break a hole in your heart,
let the heart feed.

For Charlie Beaulieu in Yellowknife Who Told Me Go Back to the South and Write Another Poem About Indians

Afterward when we climbed out into the
black hills like two small outlaws determined
to live, the smile on your face provided no
camouflage.

You showed me the village where your mother had
lived, a glint on the horizon like a mirror

tilted in sunlight to guide you safely back.
Not your own mother, you told me, but
an adopted one. They killed her with cheap wine and
took off without paying anything.

Your father was hunting. When he came home
her face was fat as a beer barrel.
He cut off her head and buried it in a sack.
The police claimed the rest of the body.

Later while you gathered food, I picked flowers.
The foxtails and the fireweed made a perfect bed.
I did not ask for words this time, or forgiveness,
or even a dream to help me sleep.

That morning I had seen you shoot an arrow
three miles over the lake. Whatever you hit
died. Together we rowed out as if
some bond had been made; all day I grew stiff
under your bright shadow.

That night I was cold when your quick fingers
cut into me, picking the choice bits.
There was no way to stop the bleeding then,
or the stench of my last supper. You wrapped
each piece carefully, my heart among them.
Thirteen red bundles. You laughed as I counted.

You made me whole at last. I was breathing lightly
though you held up my lungs as if to prove I was
only pretending. Blood spilled over my face, onto
my pale hands. My eyes had filled up
with something we would call tears but
weeping, you told me, was part of another ritual.

Then you put price tags on all my bones,
souvenirs for summer trade.
I understood then that I did not own anything,

not even the past though there were some crimes
I could not deny easily.

I wanted to make peace but you said
there were no survivors. You spat on your
skinning knife, beginning to make progress.

A Man from France

He's a dancer
he makes you wild

he dances the dance of
lonely women

he's a deserter.

I lived with him
he made me smile

that was enough for me
but not enough for those
French ladies.

Bitches, they were brought up
differently.

They wanted a man to marry,
a man to bury.

They didn't want Harry.

Then There Was the Week

Then there was the week before
the wedding. Face it, I was
poorly armed against all their

crowbars and leverings. My position
was not enviable.

It was a treacherous affair;
you learned to respect cruelty.
I made the most traditional bride.
Everyone was grateful.

Then there was the weekend
after the wedding. Face it, I have
strong feelings sometimes.

Then came the process of the actual
training. No sooner had I started to eat
than whatever it was began to squirm about.
It was a lesson in middle-aging.

I remember it now—that anniversary.
Everyone was grave. I hadn't yet
desired children—they said I
deserved some.

Then there was the week before
the week before the
week and then there was the week
before the wedding.

I really had to smile when these photographs
were taken.
Believe me, I genuinely had to.

A Marriage

I have changed identities
with a dead woman. Her body
lies on the floor. When the iceman

steps over her on his way to the cooler
he sees I am weeping only for myself.

When the truants and the drunks come
to leer at her chintzy underwear, it is me
they are humiliating. When the photographer
finishes his crude postures and the police
have searched her wardrobe full of crass
impersonations, it is I who stand naked before them.

When the father in his sickbed
dies of a stuck lump in the gut
and the mother is a slow black fade
in the release print, then I am like the child
in the grip of a final love scene
knowing the innocence of her creators.

When the coffin rolls up in the
middle of winter and the confused driver
stops for the right directions,
he has a photograph of someone I will not identify.
He says there can be no miscalculations;
he sees my face has grown cold and familiar.
I tell him I may have the secret he is looking for,
but clues so often lead to nothing.

I have changed identities with the
dead woman. At the funeral it is
raining hard. When they bury her the earth
is ravaged and muddy. I stare at the mourner who
stands open-mouthed and drooling but he has not come
to recognize his lover.

Later when he walks out
onto the traffic island suddenly lit up
by an accident, I am lonelier than the stranger
who has gone with my own name into the ground.

If Any Person Knows of Any Reason

Only after a lifetime of silence
did their voices speak out against me.
Forgive me I said to the jaded congregation,
to my healthy *fiancé*, to his podgy witnesses.
For a moment I had not promised anything but
vows. *I'm going to try and confuse everybody,*
delude everybody, use
everybody.

Only after the invariable ceremony
did the voices begin to whisper.
Forgive me I said on postcards to
chance relatives, to pickpockets on the
reception committee, to sweaty shop assistants.
For a while I had not dared to speak of
discipline. *I'm going to have to accuse everybody,*
exclude everybody, abuse
everybody.

After a lifetime of amputations, of desultory
skulduggery, only then did the voices begin
to whimper. Forgive me I said to the
much-featured executioner. Forgive me
I said to his audience. Nobody saw what I was
talking about; nobody heard the silence.

Forgive me I said to the priest, to the
leering crucifixion. Forgive me I said to the
derelict walls, desecrated by my own creations.
Forgive me I said to my children
whose unborn heads complained of no direction.
Forgive me I said to my old mirror: *I want to try*
and forgive everybody.

Only after a lifetime of silence
did their voices begin to assure me.
The years went by, the grave retained a cool
dead image. Forgive me I said to my own shadow
though it no longer trusted to follow.
What is it I once promised myself?
Forgive my asking.

Cursed

This love, an iron lung.
This purity, a disease to
eliminate parasites.
This patience demands time.

I speak of your heart
entombed in the vulture's gullet.
I speak of your brain
served up as pudding in a small dish.
I speak of your skull
peeled out of your skin like a
pithless fruit.

Time enough.
You have all the time in world.

Cursed, all of you, cursed.
With no hope of a cure.

This faith, a locked casket.
This humility, a cemetery for dogs.
This industry represents time.

I speak of your eyes
gouged out of the depths of the
boiler room.
I speak of your hands

crushed under the keyboard of your
identity.
I speak of every individual finger
warped into the thumbscrew of
pliability.

Time enough.
You have all the time in the world.

Cursed, all of you, cursed.
With no hope of a cure.

This joy, a mass burial.
This charity, a prayer for the
collapsed altar.
This generosity takes time.

I speak of your lips
engulfed in the mouth's cavity.
I speak of your brain
discarded on the butcher's hook.
I speak of your voice
gunned through the
emptying chambers.

Time enough.
You have all the time in the world.

Cursed, all of you, cursed.
With no hope of a cure.

This peace, a live target.
This virtue, an instrument of
torture.
This simplicity requires time.

I speak of your body
mangled in the dangling stirrup.

I speak of your bones
stewed into soup for inquisitive pigs.
I speak of your ghost
choked on its own leavings.

Time enough.
You have all the time in the world.

Cursed, all of you, cursed.
With no hope of a cure.

When He Decided He Was Finished

to prove his love
he sent a severed hand.
She imprisoned it
in a bottle.

To show his concern
he tied himself up in a sack
and threw his body
into the ocean.

She made a changeling out of wax.
She tucked it under her skirts.

To prove that he
understood freedom
he killed his pet bird.
She made a nest for it
amongst thistles.

He began to have feelings
of confusion.

To prove his need
he cut himself into small pieces

with a dull knife.
She was already a ghost;
he grew less assured.

The moon like a prickly burr
brushed against his heart.
She crucified a cat
and left it to bleed on his pillow.

He dressed himself in his
darkest clothes.
He called her, very gently.

He felt a pain
more permanent than defeat.

She was only beginning.

You Ghosts

turned human long ago.
Have no faith in anything.

I rise like a Christmas moon
impaled on the penis bone of a bear.
I rise for every female calving.

You ghosts are so delicate these days
it's actually quite painful.
You've lost your ability to fear anyone.

The truth is, you finished me off;
I should be gracious for such mercies.
Death was a fashionable partner once—
I had my fill of flesh.

Ah, the pity.
Ah, you.

An infected corpse in the groin.
Bog-muck in the brain.

Love, love.

I am wholly yours.

Even in the Ordered World

Always the men I love
return to the mountains.
Always they return
to their mountain women.

Always they carry
my tired smell in their hands,
my taste on their shaky fingers.
Only my innocence
ever remains constant.

Always the men I know
love cages. Their women have
sensitive claws and teeth.
At feeding time their habits are
horrible. They pick at the
red mess thinking it is meat.

I do not believe there is a place for me
in those mountains, or a cage that could
leave me lonely enough to enter.

Even in the ordered world
choices become difficult.

The men I will never stop to love
have lives that deserve
some miracle.

The Way We Were

Through the ruins of the walls
I can smell the rind of
oranges. My mouth tastes of
sweet spice and pieces of flesh.

Beside me under the covers
you are asleep. Discarded
scraps of iron litter the floor.
Now is not the moment
for reconciliation.
You are content dreaming of
hot and lazy women.

The reporters along the corridor
are eager for another day.
The telephone goes off like a gun.
I rinse my knife and stagger
into town.
Later, down by the breakwater,
I start humming the same old tune.

Photo by Doane Gregory

Cocktails at the Mausoleum
1985

I. Coming into Town, Cold

Paul and the Full Moon

The night is cool.
Love takes us and changes us
so that even the moon is always
rising—it rises behind your eyes
where I see things enter and grow.
There is a light around your body,
a pale delicate light that makes
everything seem brighter.
It's a strange light and at times
it makes touching you impossible.

I touch you.
The light comes from inside you,
from a place that even the moon
cannot reach. You pull me there
with all your knowledge of darkness.
I come, I stay. In this light
I could easily be blinded.

I know that. So sometimes when
we touch I start to feel afraid.
You know it too, and cover up my eyes,
but the moon shines through your skin
and I feel it enter me.
I am surprised; I have never shared
this moon with anyone. Later,
much later, you give me the whole sky.

The Plane Put Down in Sacramento

and we headed for the foothills
on a Greyhound bus. It was hot,
there was nothing to say. We hadn't
even planned to come this way together.

Years ago I made the same journey
from Sacramento into the foothills
looking for adventure. I was thirteen
and that summer my godmother taught me
how to cook. I wanted to pan for gold
instead, run wild into the mountains.

I remember deep pools in a clear
mountain stream, and lying beside a boy
who said he loved me too much.
We didn't touch, he loved me that much.
I ached, I wanted him all afternoon.

Afterward I confessed, confused by my
feelings. My godmother said I was oversexed;
all summer long I went on needing.

I think you must have been with me then,
I think you have always been with me.
There's something of you in everyone
I've loved. There's something in you
that's different.

If this bus stops anywhere, we'll get out.
You say you want to see dolphins as the
desert rolls past. I've got sand in my eyes
and sometimes I can taste water. The desert
is an ocean, and the waves go by unbroken.

You take my hand. Your face—I've been
watching is secretly for hours—turns

toward me and you bend to kiss me.
It's the first time we've touched;
the surf breaks in my blood.

I half-believe we could travel forever,
gazing out through tinted glass and
breathing the salt breeze. The breeze
is gentle; I think I can hear dolphins.
You move your body closer.
I think I can hear them singing.

The Moon Is Upside Down in the Sky

and Paul is in Acapulco
looking for avocados.
Papayas and mangoes are ripening
in the shade; when the moon is this way
we each have hidden powers.

There are frogs in the underworld
singing of the upper air. They
want to go there, they want to
dress in women's bodies and
come to our bed bringing messages
from the spirits.

The bed is cold. Paul is in
Acapulco. Strange beautiful women
are trailing him through the streets—
they know he's not ordinary,
they want to know more about him.

They enter my sleep, like frogs,
like spirit beings; later when I wake
I don't know who I am.
The women are hungry, they wrap
their tongues around me. Their eyes

are the colour of the Acapulco moon,
their skin is like Paul's avocados.

Later we laugh about it, how
Paul was followed home and the bed
filled up with frogs. Still I'm confused;
I think those frogs were human.
Frogs wouldn't look at Paul
that way, like hot-blooded women
in town for a good time.

Coming into Town, Cold

that is, not knowing anyone
and having nowhere to go,
not speaking the foreign language either
but trying to get by on hard-earned
Canadian poetry royalties.

Miami was a disaster. I lost
my pen and my American Express Card
(one an omen, the other an inconvenience).

Paul says I shouldn't be superstitious
but he's not here right now. It's mystical
out there where he is. I would quit tomorrow
but there is still his body to be reckoned with.

I'm glad I'm not in Miami
though I slept through most of the week.
There's no place for poetry in a world
like that, and furthermore I met no one
who'd even heard of Vancouver.

In Panama I'll learn Spanish
and soon I'll have someone to talk to.
An address, maybe, where friends can write,

and one day a house with a view to
South America.

Nothing is ever enough—the thought
creates panic. I'm over twenty-nine and
only inertia stops me from considering suicide.

Paul, if he were here, would provide another
reason. When we're naked or just rising
half-naked above the bed, I can't even remember
which continent we've left.

Taking You to the Airport

in your white suit
and your python boots

leaving you there and driving home
in the old vw
with the accelerator pedal sticking.

Rain comes through the floor
there's no more I can do

giving and taking,
just getting through.

But you are out of my arms
and into another airport—
I want to hold you and bring you
back down, back into my arms,
down to the ground.

Your love is safe with me,
I want you to know.
When you leave take me with you—
let me go.

Supposing You Have Nowhere to Go

supposing you have no one.
Supposing the person you love is in
Panama, has been away for weeks
and you don't know how to find him.

At night in the house all things are crying—
the teapot, the clock radio, the things
you rely on. The mirror stares back at you
from a distance that makes breathing impossible.
You see nothing but empty shadows, and these
have the faces of strangers.

Supposing you go to town, you meet and
talk with friends but they too have become
strangers. Your family invites you home
but when you arrive they no longer know you.
Supposing later, when you drive down the
highway, even your own house has abandoned you.

Supposing this happens when you are
twenty-nine; supposing it happens this way.
All your life you have never belonged
and suddenly you are nowhere.

You pull up your favourite chair, you sit
alone in the garden. You count, very slowly,
the number of times your heart beats in a minute
—supposing it beats forever in the emptiness
of your body? Supposing you stop counting and
no one is there to notice. Supposing then
that the one person who might have cared
comes walking toward you, hangs his head
and is silent.

My Pirate Came Back from Bogotá with Powder Burns on His Leg

and a .38 in his briefcase
and a pocketful of lead.

Afterward we drank orange juice
and talked about emeralds

there was a moon, I remember,
a cold slit in the sky,
and a war going on in Ecuador
and another in Guatemala.

Later, tired of talking,
we made love. I think it was
on the roof of the Hotel
Conquistador, I think it was
all we had left to do
given the night and the
thin moon which, when fatter,
lacks the same power.

You pressed yourself into me,
tired of living alone.
There comes a time when you
tire of a life together,
but that comes later still.

I remember I was thinking
how longing becomes regret
when you pressed yourself so hard
that a bullet bore into me.
It left an impression on the
inside of my thigh, as below me
in the doorway a blond girl
kissed a black man goodbye.

She had her face turned
upward to the sky where her
eyes burned like my triggerhand
to pull and unload the
murderer in the heart.

You held on to me as if you thought
love could last forever.
The blond girl left with her
poodle in a cab.

Hunchback on the Buga Road

Stopping beside a place where the
pine trees grew wild and straight as
children, I saw her cower and shrink
from the flowers in the ditches
as if she knew beauty
was something to be ashamed of.

I saw her face.
The children who came out of nowhere
tried to step on her shadow;
it was good luck, they told us,
to step on the hump.

She was singing a small song,
of possibilities and roads not
taken. Of laughter and clear nights
and a man she had somewhere forgotten.

At least I thought that's what
she sang. Out of her sight we
stopped for a picnic, and picked flowers
that were too beautiful. They died
in the trunk of the car that night.

In Buga. We made love under
a clear sky, in the shadow of the Andes,
and afterward I started singing—
do you remember how you used to laugh?
I sang the old woman's song again,
at least I think I was singing.

No matter; it was years ago.
I've learned to speak her language and
I know now what she was saying. She sang
"Can't reach where it itches." Only that.
I wish, at the time, you had told me.

Cali

Wind comes through the canyon,
a soft wind with
no name or direction.
It lights upon your eyes like
wakening birds

and love, once something so small
and ordinary, touches me.

Sir Lionel Luckhoo, Listed in the Guinness Book of Records as the World's Most Successful Advocate with 228 Successive Murder Acquittals, Humbly Lays His All at the Feet of Jesus

There I stood in the rain
black skirt hitched up high and a
hint of lace at the neckline when someone,
Jesus it seems, smiled down on me,
opened his large good arms and
offered me his deck chair under the tarpaulin.

I walked up to that deck chair
with little faith in anything,
quite ready to turn my back on life completely
but fearing the inexorable conclusion.

I admit I was impressed by his
impeccable manners, old heartthrob he
with teeth flashing.
Like daggers of bone, that smile hit home—
he was a shark feeding on cool wedges of
sunset and dark eyes flashing under the jacaranda.

I admit I was feeling divided—
the fish of my flesh could easily have fed a
multitude—when Sir Lionel arrived in his
chauffeur-driven Mazda.
Jesus skipped the reception line to mix with the
common people while I sat there watching,
confused by a spectacle that others seemed
to be taking for granted—the crippled rising up
and dancing, the blind unbandaging the injured.

Wine flowed like blood from the throats of the
flowers while birds sang from the trees.
The sun and the moon shone at once in the
same sky, and all the stars became butterflies,
frail and dazzling.

Sir Lionel looked amazed; he quickly adjusted
his cufflinks.
When his voice was raised his words were barely
audible; for the first time in his life he had to
compete for an audience.

But when the dust had settled over all the
bright dancers, and the stars were only stars
again in a sky that loomed over us as if in
final judgement, Sir Lionel led the crowd

in prayer, and left shortly afterward
with Jesus in the Mazda.

The crowd followed.
So much for me, all sudsy heart and soul—
I was left sitting there.
I had to make my own way home:
the way was clear and I went alone.

Ordinary People

After two years of torture, he said,
he couldn't touch a book of poetry
without trembling.
They let him go because he was the
wrong person—after two years of torture
he could not say *I love you*
to his wife or his children.

His torturers, he said, were
ordinary people—they had feelings too.
Sometimes they would show him photographs
of their families—ordinary people
like me, like you.

Personally I do not like to
think about torture. I do not like to
hear of it on the radio, or read about it
or even believe it happens.
I know it happens.
He told me, after two years of torture
you still can't believe it's happening.

You just want to die but
they won't let you. If you happen to die
they have a real sense of loss.
Torturers, he said, have feelings too.

They are ordinary people
like me, like you.

The Unconsidered Life

No one can shut out
the shamelessness of the body,
or love the discipline of torture
and remain faithful.

No one can shut out
the sadness of the body,
the need of desire
to grow and rot.

Every time it is the same
thing, always the scales tip
for the innocence of guilt.
Always I have no curative powers.

I am the bride with
worms around her heart
and a skull bursting with goodness
like a church goblet.
I am the bearer of accused children.

No gallantry can ease
the painfulness of the body
or understand the camouflage
to celebrate its loss.

Death is nakedness
suddenly become flesh.
Suicide is pornography.

Hurt Birds, Vultures and B-52s

helicopters, too, over the
Bridge of the Americas.
Where the sky bends it bleeds,
meets shark-infested water.
We make love at the water's edge,
ignoring the dead soldiers.

They grow stiff inside their
duty pants, their heads picked
clean as bullets. We could
plant flowers in this difficult
spring, affirm our belief in
something beyond the future.

At least it doesn't rain here
like it does in the country we've
come from. At least we have
each other to hold, though how
through this pain can
loving keep us together?

Like hurt birds in a cage
we learn to accept the loss.
It's safer to stay
where the vulture is only an image.

For the planes descend and the
love goes out of us.
From where we are lying we can
sense their fear—it drives us
into our own bodies and
there we become strangers.

We are tired, too, and the tide
has risen beyond us. We embrace

as if it's not happened before,
a hopeless conceit, but human.

The Shark Came Up

out of the water onto the
beach, a freak marriage of
flesh and air with terror
a gimmick to capture the
crowd's attention.

I was just sitting there
with various organs missing,
an oddity myself
having so far managed to
appear quite ordinary

when the shark singled me
out, sliced through the
heart's cavity, through the
hole that is, where pieces
of my heart were missing.

But oh I had teeth too
and a weird thirst for my
own blood, and there was
nothing that shark knew
I didn't know better.

We conspired and soon
we rolled up the rug;
athlete and intellect
we had that beach crawling.

I suppose it's an art,
the act of maiming,
and for one complete moment
I felt like a creator.

Then the crying began
and the terrible craziness.
I stayed while the shark swam
away; the art of survival was
something he understood better.

But the dying wanted reasons
where the grave was reason enough
and all I could do was to toast the
shark as the mob moved in to
reconcile our differences.

The sad event would alter
nothing—no laws or fears or
complicated griefs. They dragged
my body onward to the sea.
The shark came to greet me
cradling his oily genitals.

II. Second Sight

Yesterday and Today

I am the girl in gazelle horns
and a torn nightdress.
I have no body.
See, nothing hurts.

Yesterday it snowed.
I lay down making a large good angel.

Today it thawed.
Another looked out through her small
blind eyes, crying

whose horns are those,
whose torn clothes?

Second Sight
for Marilyn

The flies were thick in the bush
and we had nothing but trouble.

Our clothes were uncomfortable;
like sleepwalkers we stripped
and spread wide our arms

it was misty and cool

our eyes could not focus on
details

and everywhere the smell of the
wild, wild roses
assaulted our senses.

We found a clearing and built a
fire.
We were two little sisters
and life together was awesome.

Being born into that wide, cool,
misty, wild rose morning

we touched each other and a
bear came.
A bear came running with a crowd
after him,
a black bear with a secret black hole
in his heart.

We wanted to help.
Two sisters we believed in sharing

and called him to our human fire,
content with caring.

He was an ugly bear,
unused to kindness.
He did not forgive us
but embraced us.

Two old gaping women we
still remember that touch

and try to recall the vision
in words:

an old bear echoes
enough, enough!

J Took a Wire Cage into the Woods

I took a wire cage into the woods
in which to sit and watch the animals.
They gathered round me as I'd hoped they would
and sat, expressionless, with closed eyes,
warming themselves in the sun.

Their bodies were beautiful, unlike mine;
their bodies were solitary, never lonely.
They must have sat for hours in one place
as if to reassure me all was understood.

Their patience was exhausting. All night
I watched till dark and light were
blotted out and whole seasons passed.
I did not leave that cage again but lay
under the cool influence of the stars,
awake and dreaming.

My dreams were always the same.
Always in my own image those animals rose
out of the dust, animals with human faces
whose eyes were open, sorrowful.

Their bodies were broken.
No longer content to sit and stare
at one such as this, confined by choice
within the shadows of a spectral cage,
they paced as those condemned, and wept,
while I, the guilty one, was saved.

"He Only Wishes They Would Hear Him Sing"

Conrad is slipping away.
What can I say—
he's as good as dead
and doesn't seem to know it.

Or doesn't show it.
It happens to everyone—
soon I won't have anyone.

Richard's come from Venice
for the funeral,
Jenny from south London.
Delays, delays—
Conrad is sleeping,
he's slept all day.

His wife says, "It's time.
He really should be going."
I think she wants him to go.
He won't know the difference anyway.

He is better dead—
that's all there is to say.
No one will save him.
He won't be saved.

Eaglet Tricks
after Ted Hughes

The first trick is being born
not easy to grasp, no,
the grip being difficult at
dizzying altitudes

the appetite hideous.

A voluptuous gluttony,
a gorging on flesh;
the eventual intimacy of
earth and death.

I guffaw.
The sky is evidence of my unalterable existence,
my leavings are a different matter
my judgement, law.

Unarguable I ascend
all wingbone and talon,
a flick of a bird only
the quirk of a cranky brain.

The trick is old,
the art unaccountable and infinite.

The blood moves sluggishly
through a drudgery of veins
till death, infective,
replaces pain with dull efficiency.

A Tree Wouldn't Just Uproot Itself

Today I found a severed head
lying beside a tree. The tree
had been cut down it seemed
by someone who came to me in a dream.
She said she had nowhere to live
anymore. She looked like me.

Where does a person go, I mean
after losing her head that way.
The tree was my favourite, and
as a child,
I could climb higher than anyone.

Black Mummy

has a hairy belly
a snatch made of jelly
a chest full of surprises.

Black Mummy has a gorilla
his name is Goliath
he lives up inside her
he catches spiders.

Black Mummy has a greedy pussy
it's very juicy
it's a blackberry pussy.

Black Mummy has a dolly
it looks like me
it has no body
it's a funny dolly.

Blackberry Mummy
lives in my tummy

344

I have no feelings
I cry anyway.

Jerusalem

It's a strange place to go,
but then millions do, I guess.
For two nights I've been dreaming
and dancing—flights leave every day
and something keeps whispering of it
over and over.

Think of the poor world, Jeffrey,
if only we could make the world work.
We're not the first to have felt
this way; the thing is we feel
small, not wanting to sleep but to
lie down wonderfully together

and believe in something.
I suggest Jerusalem, flights
leave every day. You say no,
think of the hordes, we don't need
a holiday, and neither of us religious.

But I was thinking of change—
only that—how to make something whole,
keep it drifting and uncertain.

You want to stay home:
it's Christmas, you say. As usual
we'll hang our stockings, side by side.
Someone, you or I, will fill them.

Tamara Went Braless to the Vatican

right under the Pope's nose
in a see-through shirt and skintight breeches.
You could hear the hosts of angels
arguing over the telescope, while others posed
eagerly with Instamatic cameras.

Such overexposure! The priests put down their
pocketbooks and prayed for darkness while the
nuns stood speechless and a limp hand
led the choir. The choirboys had hot dreams
and prayed for other miracles. Sinners confessed
to unnamed crimes.

A sign of the times. Outside the gates
women of all ages tore off their hats and
unbuttoned blouses. Hemlines became obsolete
and legs swung free as pythons. The sky itself
was dazzled and, higher up, teeth were gritted.
Breasts and buttocks made front-page spreads
and the Pope retired early to contemplate.

Angels and saints hooted—stars popped like
corks and champagne rained until all was
heavenly disorder. Tamara, in hot pink, made
mince out of the clergy. She was thinking, too,
of the boy she'd finally left, and the
heavy gold crucifix he'd given her.
She'd tossed it away while dancing
up the steps. She needed the freedom to travel.

Three Witches Go for Lunch in Elora

Driving into Waterloo on a Wednesday,
the air smells of roast pig. In Conestogo

I pass a barn that burned down during the
night, and later, in the paper, read that
five hundred pigs were killed.

Rikki and Jane saw pig ghosts in the
sky, unfavourable omens floating like
plump ions over my office at St. Jerome's.
They saw a dead cat, too, at the side of the
road, and a crow strutting with bad news from
home, the sudden death of a friend.

This little pig stayed home.
My husband won't eat pork because once,
in Science, they left a pork chop sitting
all night in a bowl of milk. By morning
the worms had emerged, leaving the pork-chop
frail as a doily. My mother said *cooking it
kills the worms*, and always overcooked the
Sunday joint.

Driving out of Waterloo with Rikki and
Jane to Elora for lunch we see them in the
distance—five hundred overcooked pigs
out for an afternoon gallop. The sky,
in fact, is full of them, fiery-eyed
insomniacs with a cold-blooded lust for women.

Hot damn says Jane.
We hoof it.

III. "We Come This Way but Once"

"We Come This Way but Once"

A poetry reading tour of England, Wales, Scotland and Paris with
bill bissett and George Johnston, October 25–November 9, 1980

I

I don't know how they keep
this train on the tracks
the wheels turn and that's it
in two weeks
bill will be chopping wood
in the Cariboo, I'll be
down in the Panama and George
back with his family.

I don't know how they keep
this train on the tracks
with all the distractions
they have to face daily.

I've been faithful to Paul
for nearly six weeks
it's not exactly easy
in fact it's a record.

I don't like sleeping alone
at night I like to hold someone.
When I start to dream about
old relationships, then it is
especially difficult.

bill says you have to wait
two years in between
major relationships
I've been waiting a few weeks
and already I'm impatient.
I don't know how they keep
this train on the tracks,
the wheels turn and
that's it.

The men along the line are
smoking, talking
bill says "in two hours
I can smoke." I don't know
how he does it.

I don't know how anyone does.
I just want to hold someone and
right now it's not possible
it never is when you
really want to   there is no one
there is really no one.

The wheels turn and
that's it   the train
stays upright, it's designed
like this.

The men along the line
are hunched against the cold
I watch them   they watch me
George says the cold is
piercing.

Yesterday at church I got
a message on my palm;
bill saw it and touched it.
bill got a message, too;

Mrs. Peel, the healer, saw
a question in his life.

In Vancouver one time I saw
a question mark on the mountain.
I was upstairs holding some
TV personality, my life
was on the line, I changed,
that was it

there clearly was, that day,
a question mark on the mountain,
and now on my palm, and in
bill's life.

But last night when we talked
I wrapped myself in his words
and there I wasn't cold anymore
I wasn't scared or lonely.

Later I had a dream—we moved to
Arizona. bill and I could actually
go there; George, of course, could
bring his large good family.

II

In yellow Wellingtons I went
to Sylvia Plath's grave
on a cold day in November—
bill was with me.

We'd heard she was buried in
unconsecrated ground
it's all the same now, the vicar
told us   he hadn't known her
personally.

At first we couldn't find her—
the cold was making it hard.
Maybe she did it to get warm
bill said. That must have been part of it.

I found a blue suitcase
in among the weeds—
someone had lost it or
left it behind, no doubt
a worn-out traveller. I too
would like to get rid of some
weight. I carry so much with me
and most of it unnecessary.

The grave was wild, I guess
that's good. I would not choose
a tidy grave myself—nor any grave:
the day will come when I have
no choice.

It's all the same now
standing at the grave's edge
bill with the blue suitcase
packed and matching the
blue shoes he'd worn out
with so much travelling.

We sat for hours in a pub
away from the cold and talked
of unrelated things. By that
I mean we avoided love or grief.

And high above Heptonstall
a cold moon hung in the sky,
a blond thing with a yellow rose
in its side   a funny duchess
a suicide.

III

The time I like best is
when we are alone and talking

this isn't a romance
so it's all right to laugh

I don't think I laughed once
all summer in Mexico
I didn't talk much either.
Lovers are quite serious, you say.
I agree, it's curious.

And complicated sometimes.
One woman you knew had herself
sterilized   I wonder
if that simplified anything
or simply hurt

we hide our hurt well
but this isn't a romance.

If it were a romance
and you brushed against me
the way you do now, in
friendship, it would probably
mean something. If I
waited for you to call and
you didn't, it would probably
hurt and I *wouldn't* hide it.

This isn't a romance.

Not laughing gets serious
sometimes   for instance
when you are leaving someone
or they are leaving

I mean people are always
leaving   next week
so will you

but it's all right to laugh
it's all right to laugh.

IV

The silver bracelet
bill didn't get
is still in the window

I dreamed of it again last night
I had wanted to buy it for
him and he for someone else
isn't that always how it is
I mean   as long as you live
your case is very doubtful.

You decide, say, not to live.
You think you are dying to
punish someone when really
you are dying to free them

that's a good enough reason
for staying alive

and all this over one
silver bracelet.

The bracelet was in the window
of a shop owned by Mr. Benson.
His neighbour told us he was
never open. They no longer speak:
Mr. Benson, she said, is a bit
of a twister.

We might find him at the library
where he goes to read the news.
"A single sentence will suffice
for modern man: he fornicated
and he read the papers."

That's our Mr. Benson. Hot on
his trail we hightailed it
down to the library. He was late,
it wasn't like him, said the
librarian. He wore a beard and a
black cloak—his grandfather
was a warlock.

bill searched every café (George
took the 9:06 up to Newcastle).
I thought perhaps Mr. Benson
was in bed, having overslept
or died—the ultimate sentence.

But we found him walking back
to open up his shop   he never
opened before noon he said,
but for the silver bracelet
one hundred and fifty pounds

sterling! bill was prepared to
pay around thirty   I would have
gone higher and given it to him
so that he, in turn, could
give it as a gift

but things don't actually work
like this—my case would still
have been doubtful.

The silver bracelet
bill didn't get
will always be in that window

on it a young girl and a
man who is also unattainable.

They do not touch though their
fates are intertwined.   Together
they shine   in bill's eye,
in mine.

V

"I heard some good news today."
said George. "We come this way
but once." We were on a train
between London and Brighton—
I seemed to remember having
come this way before.

It was ten years ago and the
circumstances were similar.
I was waiting to meet a man
on whom all my life depended.
He was late, I recall, or else he
never arrived. Years later I can't say
it makes any difference.

I am still waiting, there is
still no one. In the station at
Brighton I heard George Harrison sing
"I really want to see you but it
takes so long..."

Last night in Oxford I dreamed
I went blind. I was high up in the
sky; as usual I was waiting for
someone. Whoever it was arrived
but then I couldn't see him.
bill dreamed our ship was about to
go down. George dreamed, blissfully,
nothing.

In my life my dreams are the
only continuity   bill the same
though I can't speak for him.

I suspect as much   when the ship
sank he stayed with it. I, too,
though floundering. Others, around
us, abandoned the ship and drowned.

       VI

The terrible parting in
Paris or London has yet
to come, with all the sadness
rolled into one

but you can't hedge on the wheel.

Today we're together in
Glasgow. It's starting to feel
permanent; all the hotels,
the lonely stations, they're
starting to feel familiar.

In Norwich I saw a church
that had been bombed by a
Zeppelin and in Coventry the
new cathedral. By Cardiff
we were thoroughly festive.

bill was kept awake in Dundee
with the election on television
and a toilet endlessly flushing

I slept through dreams of
one train pulling away after
another

we were saying goodbye
on a platform in some station
it meant we would
stop travelling together
it meant we would go on alone
and in different directions.

George had gingercake and honey
I had a handful of rain
I said what use to anyone
is a handful of rain
I am always trying
to make sense out of things.

I want everything to last,
at least to stay the same.
bill says I should let it all go
you can't hedge on the wheel.

So I turn and the wheel
turns and the sadness turns too
into tears and laughter, the
unspeakable circuit

one train pulls away after
another and all the sadness
is rolled into one.

What use is a handful of
rain I say   away with it!
Let it go!

In Whitehorse I Wanted You

and in every other town.
All around there were mountains,
when I looked down I saw the
mountains reflected.

I saw your face.
I must have heard your name in
every place I stopped and
each day seemed the same and
each night took me further away from you.

David stood up to read his poetry.
He said every day billions of things happen
and are forgotten. For a while
his poetry made me laugh,
but then I was alone again
in another hotel room.

I tried writing you a letter, I said
Bill it's all I can do to drag myself
upstairs. I've been bawling to adolescents
the inscrutable agonies of the dead.
In my room in this Travelodge
there are two double beds.

The letter never got finished.
I fell asleep reading a book,
reading over and over *"There's a thing
he doesn't know. He doesn't know
you can't catch the glory on a hook
and hold on to it. That when you fish for
the glory you catch the darkness too.
That if you hook twice the glory
you hook twice the fear."*

All night I slept and dreamed I was
running. There was a mountain road
and flowers so beautiful I wanted to
pick them all and press them in a book.
That way I could keep them and
they wouldn't change.
I think you were running with me.

IV. Requiem for Talunkwun Island

I Want to Remember David

I want to live on the same island
as David

I want to drive down to 'Charlotte
in his '56 Buick Special
stopping along the way to pick mint
at Miller Creek and briefly
at Jungle Beach for lamb's quarters

if they're in season

I want to wait at the Landing
while David gets the clock radio going
and leaves the car on display at
Skidegate Esso
where neither the highest nor
any offer shall necessarily
be accepted.

I'll bring armloads of lilac from the
condemned house where we stayed once

I remember there was that
grand occasion when David did a dance,
a striptease for the Mounties who came to
search everyone:

David was a real shocker in
black pumps.

I want to remember David
drifting in a leaky skiff without oars

alone in the rain at the north end of the world
with a picnic basket full of love letters
from Christopher.

Josef's Ghost

is soul-travelling on the
Tlell River
spirit-dancing up the clambanks
looking for trouble.

Josef's ghost is reading
The Anatomy of Melancholy
mumbling about atrocities
swigging a Skidegate Cocktail.

Josef's ghost goes hunting with a six-pack,
picnics beside the Geikie under a collapsible
umbrella.

Josef's ghost spooks geese on the
muskeg, sabotages the underground
telephone cables.

Josef's ghost courts
young Janey Brown, leaves wreaths
on her worn front doorstep.

Josef's ghost glows in the dark,
frightens the daylights out of our daft Jamie.

Josef's ghost wears a yellow hard hat,
goes to IWA meetings and
leaves abruptly.

Josef's ghost declares bankruptcy at the
Kaien Consumer's Credit Union.

Josef's grave is a National Monument.
Louie's Harriet gives guided tours on
local holidays.

Josef's grave is cluttered with
old wrecked engines,
it is littered with statements from
used-car dealers.

The last time I saw Josef I was sitting beside
the ditched vw

and Josef hitched a ride into Port to scrounge
spark plugs and a new battery:

he was a real genius.

Vern and Joanne: Dead

and Mike Davis just back from his
holiday brings us the bad news.

Jack Miller pours another whiskey.
His old lady has left, moved to
Pouce Coupe. So far *he's* got the kid,
but there's going to be a fight.

Mike feeds the airtight,
Helen cooks the spaghetti.

"They were wiped out in a car,
I don't know how it happened."
Most likely Joanne wasn't wearing her glasses:

they'd just come from the Commune
and Brother Love says glasses are crutches.

I remember you, Vern, at Cape Ball one winter.
We swam naked in the river.
And when the time came for you, Joanne,
you too lay down naked.
Vern delivered your second baby.

Mike says your babies are safe,
they were riding in the back.
Nobody knows how it really happened.
It happened a long way from the Islands.

Helen serves the spaghetti.
That Christmas at Cape Ball we had
smoked salmon, poached that spring.
Vern, you Viking, driving your old
vw over the Cape Ball river at
high tide—you said you'd lost
three of them that way but you
kept on trying *"A good Volksy will do
300,000 miles on one engine."* And once,
broken down in the rain, you stopped to
offer me a ride.

Your deaths bring me closer to my own.
Friends die, friends go on living.
I visit the graves of my friends,
the houses of my friends.
Mike says he felt at home in the Commune;
Jack Miller says he hasn't time to
stay for dinner.

I eat my spaghetti, silently.
I think that being alive must not
mean very much.
Between mouthfuls I leaf through

Patrick's postcard collection:
Africa, Victoria, the World Famous
Sea Lion Caves in Oregon.
Some of them I recognize—they are
written in my own handwriting.
The messages are indecipherable now,
the ink already faded.

We talk of this and that.
Jack's latest artifact and the
illegality of eagle feathers in
Idaho.

And Vern and Joanne, dead.
Outside in the stillness a mad dog barks
at his own shadow.
Mike pours the wine and there is some
good cheese for afterward.

Outside in the trees a dead wind is rising.
We eat our spaghetti, silently.

We are happy to see each other after a
long summer. More whiskey for the glass
and Jack Miller says he may after all
have time, this time, for supper.

Requiem for Talunkwun Island

Talunkwun Island, named after the Haida word for phosphorus, lies in the South Moresby group of the Queen Charlotte Islands or Haida Gwaii. In recent years clear-cut logging on the steep slopes of this island caused massive erosion and landslides and has made reforestation impossible.

I

> *You need not think they will make such a continual noise of*
> *singing in Skedans Creek as they used to in your previous existence.*
> —Haida mourning song

The sad ghost of a
dead art I come
down out of the mountains.
I am weak with hunger
and my hands, oh like the
cedar trees, are stumps.

The animal inside me
sniffs the breeze.
It is all lonely darkness
breathing in and out like the
sea. Over the slick rocks at the
lip of the falls I fell
back through my father's words
and into the womb of my mother.

I almost feel whole again
remembering how it was.
I could move among the trees,
embrace heaven and rock when
gods dwelt in all places
and everything was singing.

I was raven, eagle—

I flew up up up into the top
of the salmonberry bushes.
The sky was a wilder place
in those days, wider and cleaner.
I recall you could travel
just singing and flying,
with the sea all phosphorus
lighting the way below.

Now I sit and stare at
the ocean. Sometimes for days I sit
and watch. Who hears the songs
when the voices are silent?
Who remembers the great sound we used
to make, on the shores of an island
we thought would last forever.

II

> *What do they think they will attain by their ships*
> *that death has not already given them?*
>
> —William Carlos Williams

The submerged rocks sleeping like
whales did not stop them,
nor the winds that beached our
canoes and sent the
kelp gulls crying inland.
We thought their sails were clouds
and how could we have known better.
The sky was overcast and black;
my old grandmother picked cloudberries
and hid them under her hat.

The ships had come to trade—
what wealth we had was little then,
and nothing now.
My mother had to go begging

that winter. A young girl she grew
quieter and older.

If my hands were good I would
carve her something—the moon
gripped in a raven's beak—
but where would I find wood enough,
or the right spirit.
I lit a fire instead and stood in the
coals. A ship sailed out
and darkness tossed the sleepers
from its hold.

I felt tears on my young face
like rain down a mountain rock.
Something was lost; I could feel it
as I followed a deer trail to the
seacoast.

It was a day's journey
but it took me all my life.
At the end I found a highway
and people living in houses.
The trees were cut down and the
land had been sold for a pittance.
The old names were gone and the
ravens, for once, were silent.

I took the eyes of an owl
and stitched them into my head.
I took the wishbone of a foetus
and pressed it into my breast.
I sailed up into the clouds
and blackened the sky with earth.
The sky would mourn, too, the way
death does, in the roots.

III

But they could die for years, for decades,
so tall their silence, and tell you nothing.
—Howard Nemerov

They were sacred.
Their silence was something we
lived by, not the noise of machinery
stripping the thickets.

The trees were our spirits;
they have gone into nothingness.
They have become mortal, like us;
we diminished them and they have become
human.

Eternal life is unlivable
yet men rut like fat bucks in the
bush and women go on sighing.
It's a sad thing to be lonely in the
body, but to have no body at all—
that's the loneliest.

If I had the penis bone of a bear
I would point it at that woman.
Now there are no trees left to
shelter us, and the grass where we
could have lain is withered
and unyielding.

I wish there could be forests upon
the earth again, a place for our
children to gather. I wish the trees
would return during our own lifetime,
take hold and grow that we might
live again under their silence.

Now men talk of the wood they must
carry, they speak of the weight in
tired voices. I remember a time
when the whole world was singing,
and a love that kept us bound
by things we could not know.

IV

> *The wind blows where it will, and you hear the sound of it,*
> *but you do not know whence it comes or whither it goes,*
> *so it is with every one who is born of the Spirit.*
>
> —John 3:8

They took my hands
and threw them into the ocean.
I saw them scuttle toward Skidegate
like white crabs with supernatural power.

It is sometimes necessary to sit
and say nothing,
to watch what takes shape,
and changes, out of that silence.
It is sometimes a necessary violence.

They left my skull, I suppose
it told them nothing. My eyes had seen
the rivers full of fish but now the eyes
were older and, like the rivers, empty.
The salmon have gone elsewhere to find
their origins. Like the ghosts of my
people, they have no country.

In my chest there is something that
hurts. It once was a heart
but now it's a hole and their
fingers are eager to probe it.
I cannot tell them how life is when the

soul has left it; the body does not die
but how can they know that.

They do not remember why they were born.
They only hope to find mercy.

V. Sleeping Together

You Are on Some Road

Sometimes I forget your face,
the days erase so much of what
was never possible, but is
and is somehow permanent.

You are on some road.
A telephone rings in an empty room.
Sometimes I forget your voice,
the simple things, the certainties.

Sometimes it is too clear.
There is only distance between us.
No measure of love makes distance
reducible, the miles erase
so much of what is possible.

You are on some road.
A telephone rings in an empty room.
Sometimes I am certain; you are leaving,
it is permanent. Sometimes it is simple,
it is only distance.

Beginning Again

Nothing resolved, we set out.
It was Sunday, raining, you said
I can't know you.
I don't.
No one does.

You lived on a mountain
you tell me that much.

The mountain had a name

tell me what it was.

A Feat of Arms

I slept with war
all night I slept with war once.
I did not sleep peacefully
but killed without guilt whatever it was
I needed.

There are wounds you never wake from,
wounds that lie silent under an enemy
of skin.
There are desperate wounds
that keep you alive for hours.
They stick to you for days.
You can't heal them.

There are costly tombs on the
perfect grass
and lonely flights through drunken spaces
with nothing to pray for and
no one to listen.

It's a rut.
It's drab.
I'd like to go somewhere.

I'd like to find something worth being
wounded about
and sleep without comfort forever again.

Sleeping Together

In my dream you have become
a fisherman. You are going fishing
in my sleep.
"Sharks come to light and blood,"
you whisper, as if you have always been
a fisherman. A shark surfaces beside me;
still I cannot stop dreaming.

In your dream I am a bird,
I am trapped inside your house.
I flap my wings, beat on the windows.
"My house has no roof," you say.
Still I cannot get out.

You touch me, very gently,
You want to make me happy.
You say so, over and over.
You want me to stop dreaming.

In your dream I am dead.
You have made sure of that.
Still I am stronger than you
and more confident.
My hand does not tremble as yours does.
when you twist, again, the knife.

In my dream you have become an
undertaker. You are siphoning my blood
under a cold light.
"Sharks come to light and blood,"
you whisper, as if you have always been
an undertaker. Still I go on dreaming.

You touch me, very gently.
You want me to make you happy.
You want me to stop dreaming.
You say so, over and over.

A shark is swimming toward us;
still, we sleep.
"Stop dreaming," you whisper; he surfaces
beside me.
"Stop dreaming," you shiver; he nudges your
blind windows. The shark has become a bird,
like me. Trapped inside your house we are
flying, flying.

"My house has no roof," you cry,
but the shark, too, is dreaming.
Like me, he does not want to stop dreaming.
He does not want to stop dreaming.

Somewhere You Are in the World

Somewhere you are in the world
and I am not.
You let me go and I left;
having come this far
I cannot speak of the distance.

A world lies between us.
All day I talk with men whose lives
are orderly; they want to hold me but

not touch. This time last week we were
lying in your bed.

There was a map of the world
on your wall—it covered a hole, you said.
Our bodies made that world seem small
but now I am lost in it and
you are somewhere else.

I stare out the window,
I drive into town, walk around.
Life is ordinary; I write you letters.
I tell myself it is a matter of time,
I tell myself there's no urgency.

Today I found that book on boatbuilding;
tomorrow I'll buy rosewater at the market.
These are the things you wanted
and I'll send them. If they reach you
write to me, or call me long distance.

You see, the world hurts;
without you I too am lessened.
It happens when I reach for you
and no one is there.
You see there is really no one.

"Exile Is in Our Time Like Blood"

You are beautiful: it hurts me.
All knowledge of you is pain
and after that knowledge is nothing.

I know you.
You take me and I change.
I break from your body
make with our lonely bodies one flesh, love,
and that enough alone.

I fill up my days with you
my nights are filled up.
Something I am grows emptier
something I am holds on and will not let go.

Time passes, only just.
You are more and more beautiful: it hurts.
Each time I reach for you something is lost;
something is born again
over and over.

One Day in Winter

That's how it was.
The black pond stank
and the leaves shivered
and the dead man swinging from the
branches of a bare tree
was cold when I found him,
very cold indeed.

I touched him.
I knew him.
All day long my hands
smelled of him.

That's how it is.

And when you reached for me later
I wasn't there.
When you touched me again
I was nowhere.

Day After Day

I don't know where you go
but when you are gone

the animal that I am
lies down and is silent.

The world is white,
small. I can't live in it.
It takes you away.
You choose to go
where you know I cannot follow.

There is no choice.
We take from each other
what can never be shared

I rise, you rise,
into the empty arms of morning.

Gone

The door closes
and then you are nowhere.
I try to follow but
all doors open inward and
you are not anywhere.

Somewhere in the darkness
you are waking

and when I come running
it is to hold you
I want to hold you.

The streets are empty
I am running toward you
toward something I don't know

I can't stop
can't wait to touch you

but the door opens
and then I am not anywhere.

Somewhere I am walking
and the dream has no ending

above me, all clouds and stars,
the sky has no beginning.

It is like this in the evening,
when we wake together;

lying still
our bodies are certain

we are seasons with no names
embracing all weathers.

Your breath on my lips is dry,
is burning.
You remember that thirst
like the first time you
tasted water.

Your Daughter

We drove through an old rain
after not speaking for a week.
I cried when you left

cried and cried for the words
not said.

We never believed in them.
Father, lover, we were stranded,
were islands.

Your daughter rode toward us on a
horse. Your daughter who walks
like me, with a slight stoop,

and cries, too, when you leave her.

"& the great white horses come up & lick the frost of the dream"

I touch your cold face,
your closed lips and eyes.
I touch the dead place in the
bed, the place where you still lie.

"Did you remember to feed the horses?"
you say, suddenly rising.

Of course the horses.

You dreamed   they died.

When J Stopped Loving You

we went out walking.
I was a whole new world inside,
alive and bending.

You picked thimbleberries,
one for each finger.
Nimble, we mended.

Something, not death, is faithful.

"And on the Coming of the Outrageous Dawn"

I want you to
come to my bed,
I don't know you.
I know your eyes—they
depend on the sea. I don't
believe in a language
that brings us closer together.

I want you to be gentle
because the world is wild.
The cool light of the moon
can look on weakness and
never falter.
I've seen you in darkness
defying the moon's skill.
You remain whole and golden.

I want you to
come to my bed, I want you to
come slowly. Forget what you
left or why I returned,
forget that we ever were lonely.

Holding you is like
letting something go;
knowing this, I need you.
Now your eyes reach for me,
join us, speak of children.
Turning to you, I embrace them.

VI. My Boots Drive Off in a Cadillac

My Boots Drive Off in a Cadillac

Always when I am dreaming
my boots, with my socks inside them,
drive off in a Cadillac
and I have to go barefoot
looking for nightlife.

The car has California plates—
I'll never forget it.
I'll never forget those boots, either.
They were handtooled in Italy.

They were always too big for me,
they slipped off easily.
I never did think they were meant for me.
They were made for someone who was
far less flighty.

The socks had a special significance,
they were given to me by a sailor.
They were a size too small but he
wanted me to wear them.
He wasn't what you'd call a sophisticated
person.

I don't know what it symbolizes,
this dream where nothing fits properly.
It's almost as if I were going around naked
or, worse, with no body at all
to make the old men wet their lips and ogle.

The men think they can buy me.
Up and down the strip I walk with a
hard line for takers—I'm no bargain.
I'm looking for a good time, a change
won't do it.
I'm dreaming of something more than a change
when my boots drive off in a Cadillac.

Remy in the Bentley

The corpse was dressed in the
back seat of the car and
I couldn't resist—I kissed him.
Right away he sat up; I could
feel his heart quicken through the
hot silk of his shirt.

My husband was asleep in the
front seat at the wheel. He is a
holy man given to easy women.
I am quite easy myself these days,
giving myself freely and for
no good reason.

This isn't a confession.
The sun was coming up and the
corpse too, for light and air,
for another shot of cognac, and,
if I'm honest, a closer look
at my cleavage.

It was the 5:30 ferry and we
were the only passengers. My
husband was reading the scriptures;
my scruples, you might say, were
about to be compromised.

The corpse was unbuttoning and
I was inclined to watch, when off
Beaver Point a fleet of blackfish
surfaced. They swam toward us like
undertakers out of the mist and
surrounding the boat they shouldered it.

Like a coffin we were carried
out beyond the islands. My husband
prayed—a calm man in a storm—while
the corpse got dressed again and
I grew increasingly silent.

For the whales, I heard them,
were singing—of their past lives
or our lives brief in passing—
I'll never know which for there
they left us stranded.

My husband prayed for wind while
the corpse and I resumed foreplay,
less earnestly than before with
an empty bottle between us.

When back into the mist, as
things will, the whales went,
black sails growing slack and
finally invisible.

I remember afterward that the
sea stayed calm, blood calm for days,
and the kelp gulls cried over us.
But always late at night we could
hear that ghostly song.
The words floated back to us like
wreaths over the gulf.

"Conversation During the Omelette Aux Fines Herbes"

I met a dead man walking in the woods today,
myself a healthy woman, barely twenty-seven.
His breath smelled of white wine and wild
strawberries—the finest white wine and the
ripest fruit.

It was intoxicating.
Our dogs gambolled together,
one black and the other white.
I told him the story of my whole life,
as far back, that is, as I chose to remember.
He wanted to know if I would be his wife—
I said under the circumstances
that would be impossible.

We reached the road that led to my house—
he kissed me, very gently.
He wanted to take me all the way,
after another kiss I agreed and invited him in
for a small meal and some light music.

One kiss more and I was on the floor
when who should walk in but my husband,
a horticulturist.
He had a cauliflower from the garden
he wanted to show me but when he saw us lying there
he said *your dog is in the garbage
fighting with another dog*

I just thought I'd mention it.

My dead man revived quite quickly,
aroused by being caught in such a compromising position.

I assured him my husband abhorred all forms of violence
and poured us each a stiff drink in the drawing room.

Your wife tells me you enjoy gardening,
our guest says, as I slip off into the kitchen to make
a good cheese sauce for my husband's cauliflower.
Small talk has never interested me
particularly.

Black Tulips

A hunchback followed me home
with an armload of black tulips,
a black hunchback with a waxed moustache—
he must have been a magician.

I say that because it was the wrong season
for tulips. The ground was covered with
leaves and just breathing I walked quickly;
the shadows were gathering like cutthroats
in the ditches.

Inside the house I felt safe from all
things though there were petals under my
covers, messages in my dreams. I think
because I missed you I noticed these things
so much. When you were asleep beside me it was
more than just enough.

But the hunchback had followed me in, it was
not an illusion. He was naked so I gave him
one of your suits, the one you never wore
that was covered with little stars.

The house suddenly changed; it felt colder
and I was a stranger. Even when he was gone

he still possessed me—I use the word possessed
because without him there was nothing left of me.

I threw out the black tulips. They smelled
of flesh, old flesh both fish and reptile,
and I think they finally died at the
bottom of the garden. I can't get rid of the
smell, it may be something permanent. You will
notice when you come back, months from now,
in your white suit cut to perfection.

You will notice the scars, too, when we are
both finally naked. In the darkness split by
lightning our nakedness should be clear to us,
but love could be there to comfort us
through the bursts of dirty thunder.

It's Easy to Be Sleazy

Orphans and widowers
they are my weakness.
Soldiers and Indians—
I've a soft spot for criminals.

They're the same after dark—
it's true—I envy them.
I could never be a lesbian
it's far too subliminal.

If I were a man
I could be a rapist.
I'd want to be obvious.
It sounds outrageous.

If you want the truth of it,
that's the thrust of it.
Love may be dead in us
but lust flourisheth.

I feel it like a disease
in the presence of my physician.
My dentist probes with confidence,
my lawyers are more reticent.

Sooner or later I'd have them all—
a pelvic missionary, I'd explore
the deepest regions of my
unexploited territories.
I'd even have time for an
animal or two, not to mention
the natives.

It's purely carnal—
there's nothing romantic about it.
Come on over to my place later
we'll have a few drinks, slip into
something more comfortable you know
and...talk about it.

John Berryman, This Is for You

Peter M. was a bit acrobatic
for my taste. He stood on his head,
did tricks in bed to please me.
It didn't do much. I left him.

I was living with George anyway.
We went to Le Touquet with Lord Lucan
and spent an amusing weekend
gambling and so on.

I left them there eventually
and took off to Ireland
(men being my main weakness)
to visit the poet Richard Murphy.

John Berryman, this is for you.
I didn't know you and I don't drink much
but I lie awake sometimes and read your poetry.
I think I know how you feel, or felt.
I feel the same way a lot of the time myself.

I had a drink with George the other night.
I think he's envious of you.
That's all there is in the end, John.
George is the jealous type.

Taboo-Man

He is fast and keeps bees
drives a flashy car
a widow on each knee

takes me voodoo-dancing
in dreams
paints his body with signs

tattoo-man

takes a hard line
ties knots in my shadow

bully-boy

I give him meat on a hook
bad blood and a butcher's curse.

I only lift up my skirt,
he grows old and mentally crippled.

I offer asylum,
I conserve spittle.

Still he wants a woman made in
somebody else's image.

I will strip naked in graveyards,
leave my body and
fly off

I will voodoo-dance in
a shallow grave
singing my own song
I will rage, rage, rage.

Taboo-man
lends me his hand

I want to marry him,
wear swamp-dock to the altar.

He wants to hurt,
likes cold women only.
Dames to rub dust into his
old wounds, old babes to
crucify him over and over.

Ju-ju man judges beauty by the
number of scars,
love by the persistence of the
infection.

Hocus-pocus man
I want your glass eye,
your good eye, too

mumbo-jumbo man
I want order.

I want dancing in my body
all down my broken body

I want to litter the beaches
with bones

long white bones of happiness
and laughter.

I want to rave.
I want to moan.

Taboo-man
I believe in you
taking and forsaking
love like you do.

Mrs. King's New Bungalow

I've slept for days in the same clothes
in Mrs. King's new bungalow.
I don't see any reason to change—
the mind might get lost in the process.

I've been dreaming most of the time—
I've dreamed about men who are
perfectly formed and naked.
There's no chance of meeting any of those types
around here—Mrs. King keeps a clean house
and more's the pity.

Ken S. says I don't like men—
he obviously doesn't understand my poetry.
He teaches English at a respectable institution
and reviews a bit.

Mrs. King won't read the papers—
that way, she says, she keeps out of trouble.
I don't blame her, it's just that I'm curious.
Ken says I don't like sex, either.

Mrs. King thinks I'm crazy—
I've slept in the same clothes for days.
If I stripped like those around me
she'd think I was making progress.
I feel more natural when I'm dressed this way.

I won't live in her house much longer,
I can picture myself in another location.
Maybe I'll give notice tomorrow.
Mrs. King will be hurt—there's no solution.

Ken says I'm fickle; I've always been the same.
I mean, I need a new man, an excuse to change.

None of that for Mrs. King—
she only had one husband.
Still she considers him a good investment—
he died suddenly.

Last night in a dream I made love to various men.
When I woke up I found Ken
making notes for a scholarly article.
He's no competition—he can't perform.
He has entered the event when
the dance is already over.

Cocktails at the Mausoleum

A name may be glorious but death is death.
—Richard Eberhart

I decided long ago that death
was not serious, if we went
anywhere else it would be less curious.
So I rode into the woods with
an outlaw and his errand boy
and drank, and made a lot of noise,
at some rich man's mausoleum.

Others had been before, revellers,
to the same place, with little care
for the monument, a vulgar Parthenon.
Of course it was out of place in
those woods, but so were we—
I would have preferred a comfortable bed
but when you ride into the arms
of an outlaw, you lie anywhere.

We lay down together.
I'm afraid the fear had gone out of me,
valuable and available I long ago
had given up my rich husband
preferring to live, if necessary, disreputably.

Here lies so and so I read, turning
my head to breathe the crushed leaves
damp beneath the ghostly boot heels:
he is dead. I heard ice cubes clink
in a glass and somebody stirring. You said
there are reasons for death
and proposed a toast to the living.

Oh, it's easy to sniff
but I did not notice when the errand boy
slipped away, nor my own glass growing empty
while I drank nothing. I was
thinking of love spent, and grief that
gropes slowly like a tendril, gnarled and
clutching over the enormous years.

Here lies so and so, his name
moss-covered though perhaps, to some,
still glorious. I decided long ago
that death was not serious, but now
with a jewelled hand something tugged,
and I felt the cold earth
rising to meet me.

It's no matter. All my life I had been
waiting for a sign, for death, too,
because I was born wanting. *There are
good reasons for death,* you said,
and sucked the spicy liquor from my
last small breath.

Boogeying with the Queen

down along the old canal
wearing an ankle-length overcoat
in spite of the heat

sucking sweets by Appointment
To Her Majesty—
the old girl got a good kick
out of that one.

You should have seen her
doing a gang-scuffle outside the
dancehall
or perfuming her body in one of the
lavatories:

she was perfect.

She was dressed for the occasion,
a crowbar up her skirt and a
quantity of quicklime.
Hard luck to the whore found dead
in a weedbed

she was queen of the quick throw
queen of alley ways.

She was beautiful and we
loved her

pockmarked with a pistol
she danced naked over our faces

queen of the underground

it felt good, good, good
to be lying beneath her.

They all loved her,
the tarts and muggers on the
commercial road.
She had a full heart for a
hatchet man, a kiss for a killer.

You should have seen her
teetering on spikes

a grudge-bearing scullion she was
obvious royalty.

When she danced we came alive,
when she danced she was really living.

There was no dance she couldn't do,
hard and fast in a small lifetime.

Just Lust

it was
only just

you were chinless
famous
shutters clicked as we
kissed

I saw the photographs afterward
and I was barely visible.

I don't make a point
of hobnobbing with royalty

it was just lust
I said, I'm a married woman
anyway.

Flustered by my common touch
you fumbled for my knee

the travelling spotlights paused,
you coughed

the orchestra played
God Save the Queen.

The Shadow of the Heart

is perhaps black
There's a fault, a crack—
nothing is appeasable

our eternal shortness of existence
ensures it.

The heart is functional,
a performer. Its shadow
eschews respectability
sings blues, sings blues

The Black Saint and the Sinner Lady
a split audience of two

heart, a tired waltz
shadow, a jazz funeral.

I got rhythm
I got rhythm

That's my nigger!
That's my nigger!

That Night on Turtle Beach

the eggs were rolling in.
I counted the dead, the newly hatched.
Slate-grey they were prey for the
lice-seized vultures.

You were proficient on the harmonica.
I was an amateur baritone.
We entertained those turtles all night
—female turtles mostly—
with a gay accordion medley.

The turtles were in a trance—
they slashed seaward.
We partied until dawn
composing tight verses to disembowelled
farm workers of both sexes.

William wrote a sonnet—
he was really a minor poet.
Maggie Laird played a bad violin solo:
her missing limbs can be found in
Los Angeles.

VII. You Didn't Fit

One More Lyric, One More
for Patrick Lane

I fail, we all fail—
that's the morality of it.
We don't know how to love,
we make a career of it.

Richard says I write in symbols,
Patrick smashes another glass.
Poetry has never been anything
but trouble. We hurt because of it.

The glass cuts; Richard says
blood is symbolic.
I say it's real.
Wounds don't heal; scars are evidence.

We don't know how to die,
we make an art of it.
Patrick says we're in trouble anyway,
it's Winnipeg, it's winter.

We don't have much to say,
words betray pain.
It's late. There's snow.
In bars up the Coast we cursed the rain.

"I Do Not Know If Things That Happen Can Be Said to Come to Pass or Only Happen"

but another year has passed
and the change is marked.
Right from the start my life stopped
making sense

at the core there was only terror,
a compass of blood in the heart's
wreckage and blood and more blood
in every direction.

It spilled out of me,
there was no reason.
As a child I buried everything
I loved, buried it down deep
and seemed pleased.

Years later the doctors
dragged it up,
opened me inside and cut the
stubborn mother from my womb.

My father rocked in his chair
unable to share his last breath
with anyone.
That was years ago when we
thought he wouldn't live much longer.
He still drives down the highway
to see me.

Ten years ago I spent Christmas
in a locked ward.
Some of my best friends
had already committed suicide.

I tried too but it wasn't in me.
The terror went deeper
where nothing could reach me.
I fell in love easily
and for no reason.
I still think, even now, I could be
more discriminating.

Another year has passed,
a decade.
Walking on New Year's Day
with friends who have survived
like me, by accident
—there is something to be said
for having such friends—
I think of the choices we made
along the way, how things
came to pass, or happened,
what brings us finally together.

The years will make sense of it.
Deep in the shadows
where the patient trees endure
and grow, a small bird rises up
out of our silence, crying
shy and wild toward open water.

You Didn't Fit
for my father

You wouldn't fit in your coffin
but to me it was no surprise.
All your life you had never fit in
anywhere; you saw no reason to
begin fitting now.

When I was little I remember
a sheriff coming. You were
taken to court because your
false teeth didn't fit and you
wouldn't pay the dentist. It was
your third set, you said none of them
fit properly. I was afraid then
that something would take you from me
as it has done now: death
with a bright face and teeth that
fit perfectly.

A human smile that shuts me out.
The Court, I remember, returned
your teeth, now marked an exhibit.
You were dismissed with costs—
I never understood. The teeth were
terrible. We liked you better
without them.

We didn't fit, either, into your
life or your loneliness, though you
tried, and we did too. Once
I wanted to marry you, and then left;
I'm still the child who won't fit
into the arms of anyone, but is
always reaching.

I was awkward for years, my bones
didn't fit in my body but stuck out
like my heart—people used to comment
on it. They said I was very good
at office parties where you took me
and let others do the talking—the
crude jokes, the corny men—I saw
how they hurt you and I loved you
harder than ever

Because neither of us fit. Later you
blamed me, said "You must fit in,"
but I didn't and I still think
it made you secretly happy.

Like I am now: you won't fit in your
coffin. My mother, after a life
of if, says, "This is the last straw."
And it is. We're all clutching.

Sometimes It Happens

The dog had been shut in the
house all day;
we were talking about love, how
sometimes it happens that you are
loved and then you are
not loved. *I'd leave him,*
you said, meaning
him, the man I love;
it's difficult, sometimes, confusing.

The dog had been shut in the
house for days.
We were talking about possibilities, how
sometimes it happens that you are
friends and then you are
not friends. *I want to,*
I said, meaning
you this time. *I told you so,*
you said; we went to bed
and the dog watched.

Years later when we woke
our families had forgotten us,
our friends had almost forgiven us.
We had children of our own,

a life where nothing else mattered.
Love, the possibilities, seemed
somehow unattainable.

You walk out later still; it is a
cold morning.
You forgot the dog, I said.
The dog is dead.

After You Left

I killed a cucaracha.
I did it instinctively as if some
arbitrary act was necessary.
I needed proof that you had left—
your absence wasn't enough. I suppose
you could say the gesture was symbolic
but this seems too obvious and
you know me better than that.

You said you'd be gone for less than
an hour but it seems to me whole seasons
have passed. The blood of the cucaracha
has dried. I covered the stain with your
new pair of shoes—cowardly, you might say,
to conceal the act.

It's complicated sometimes.
Endings are not innocent, but neither
is love or suffering. You left early,
you'll come back late. The fact that I
recently killed something will begin
to seem irrelevant.

Perhaps I won't tell you and we'll
deal with the blood in the morning.
Tonight we'll hold each other

needing only that. We'll make love
instinctively as if some
mutual act is necessary. "This is love,"
you will whisper. I'll remember it.

I Was Eating Lunch Alone in a Clam Bar in New York

when a cat came in wearing
a rat necklace.
I was in the middle of my
second week
of remembering what it felt like
to be lonely, when suddenly
I caught a scent that reminded me
of France.

The cat walked in, just in time,
upset everybody's stomach
but mine. I went out into
the street, into the rain that was
always falling, and for
the next few minutes I was
oblivious, omnipotent.

When I got home you phoned, asked
when I was coming back. I smiled
and looked at the cat, I said
*you ought to see this cat, he is
wearing a rat necklace.
He followed me.*

I stroked the cat, thinking of your
warm body in bed; the cat purred
and made much of the situation—after all
he was an outcast.

Then suddenly I was afraid, and
hung up the phone. I put the cat outside
because I wanted to love nothing,
and his scent reminded me
of a trip we'd taken to France.
We'd held each other, and we'd danced.

In the morning I found the cat,
headless outside my door.
The rats wanted their freedom too,
and they got it.

On Being Told, Ten Years Ago, Never to Use the Word "Time" in a Poem

I have eaten my glass clock.
It ticked too loudly beside the
bed where I, sleeping lightly, dreamed
of the words you left me with,
little keepsakes.

I want to call you brother
but you are other than that.
When you went away I found
my body infested with stars;
on each breast hungered a moon
and my eyes became hours
consuming the doubts of sour men.

I held my breath while the clock
wound down, but the days passed and
your letters, little bloodhounds,
found me. You loved me back;
we kept each other living.

That was the crime,
the act of letting it happen.

So when I try to recall your face,
your warm body in bed,
the clock sounds like goodbye.

It cries inside me where the
stars once raged, ragged pieces of
glass becoming part of me.
Pain thinks it can alter me but
that time has passed. Without you
I have made of love
what time cannot outlast.

I Am Not a Conspiracy
Everything Is Not Paranoid
The Drug Enforcement Administration Is
Not Everywhere

Paul comes from Toronto on Sunday
to photograph me here in my
new image. We drive to a cornfield
where I stand looking uncomfortable.
The corn-god has an Irish accent—
I can hear him whispering, "Whiskey!"

And the cows. They, too, are in the
corn, entranced like figures in effigy.
Last summer in Mexico I saw purses at the
market made from unborn calfskin—
I've been wondering where they came from
ever since, the soft skins I ran my hands
down over, that made me feel like shuddering.

I was wrong. The corn-god is whispering,
"Cocaine!" He is not Irish, after all,
but DEA wanting to do business. He
demands to know the names of all my friends,
wants me to tell him who's dealing.

I confess I'm growing restless as the
camera goes on clicking, standing naked in the
high-heel shoes I bought last summer in Mexico.
"We want names," say the cows, who suddenly
look malevolent. They are tearing the ears
off the innocent corn. They call it an
investigation.

Paul calls to them, "Come here, cows!"
though I don't even want them in the picture.
What Paul sees is something different from
me; my skin feels like shuddering when those
cows run their eyes down over me.

"But didn't you smuggle this poem into Canada?"
asks the cow with the mirrored sunglasses.
"As far as we can tell, this is not a
Canadian poem. Didn't you write it
in Mexico?"

Adrift

I was everything at once,
fish, line and lure
and small boat with person adrift in it.
I'd even go so far
as to say I was the sea.

I should describe how it felt
to be a fish pulling itself in
hooked through its own heart
by something inseparable from its flesh.

I felt confused. I felt uncertain.
When the boat rocked, I rocked too,
and when the sea turned greasy and dark
I had to roll, I was one with it.

At times I had human thoughts,
I wanted to reel in the fish and eat it.
At other times I sympathized with the sea;
I wanted to beach the boat or scuttle it.

Talk about being in two places at once—
I was in six at least. I was cold, too,
irritable in my skin and unnatural
at the end of the line. Yet, understand me,
I know how it felt to be that line,
taut and purposeful, baited in fate's hand.

It must have been you
in your little aluminum boat
who came zigzagging through a squall to
bring me to my senses. Six of them
adrift in a body with teeth chattering and

mind teetering on the brink of a
horizon which, you pointed out,
wasn't really there. You said the world
was round, not square. *Good news*, I thought,
and started rowing.

Not a Love Poem

Last night I sat in my bath
staring at the wallpaper.
The wallpaper was peeling and
I was thinking that if my bath had been
in Colombia or even Australia
there would have been cockroaches
watching me, watching me thinking
of you as I soaped my body staring
at the wallpaper

which was peeling.
Cockroaches are the worst sorts
of voyeurs. They don't see properly.
And I was thinking of you
on sabbatical in Australia
unable to write because of cockroaches
drawn to the blank sheet in your
typewriter, perhaps because of the light.

And I thought as I sat in
total darkness, the candle having
burned out

I don't blame them—
I'm drawn, too,
To the clean sheet, the mysteries.
This is one of those poems
for you.